THE ENNEAGRAM AND PRAYER
Discovering Our True Selves Before God

by

Barbara Metz, S.N.D. de N.
John Burchill, O.P.

Dimension Books, Inc.
Denville, New Jersey 07834

ACKNOWLEDGMENTS

This book is born of reflection. Enneagram Personality Theory has been part of that reflection. Yet the book could never have been written without our awareness and sharing in the faith, the struggle and the life experiences of those women and men whom we have met in our years of sharing the Enneagram. We are grateful for the sincerity of their lives and search. It has meant much to us in our personal ministry and growth. St. Paul encourages us to remember our teacher. We remember with gratitude Trevor D'Sousa, S.J. who first exposed Barbara to the Enneagram during her years of ministry in Kenya, East Africa. He planted a seed of interest that has led to the questioning and search that has made the book a reality.

Our gratitude also extends to Sr. Regina Slowe, O.S.F. for her joyful and generous offer of her secretarial skills in typing our manuscript. Our own office staff: Pamela Hamerski, Kay Walsh and Phyllis Cavan made it possible in our final crunch for us to meet our deadlines. We appreciate as well the art work for the book contributed by Sr. Pat Mullally, S.N.D. deN. To all of these people we say thank you.

ISBN 0-87193-259-8

TABLE OF CONTENTS

DEDICATION

To the staff of St. Stephen's Spiritual Life Center, Dover, Massachusetts, among whom we minister in the service of faith and goodness.

INTRODUCTION

"At various times in the past and in various ways, God has spoken to our ancestors through the prophets; but in our own times, the last days, he has spoken through his son." Heb 1:1-2

Who are these prophets that are spoken of in this text? We would like to suggest that a prophet is one who clearly names reality in the light of God's truth. This belief has, in recent years, led us to stand with humble reverence before traditions that are not our own, namely, the Judeo-Christian.

We have learned to cherish the wisdom of the East in a particular way. The Enneagram is among the treasures we have encountered.

The Enneagram study is linked in strong ways to the Moslem tradition and, in particular to the Sufis, although it is very possible that it pre-dates them.

The theory has been uncovered in recent years as men and women have delved into spiritualities that are not their own. Through workshops and some limited written materials, it has begun to be popularized.

We have been working with the theory for about five years and have wanted to use the Enneagram learning as a way of helping persons to come to a greater freedom and authenticity before God. Our desire has come from our personal witnessing of persons' struggles to find suitable ways to be present in the most basic of all relationships.

This simple, little work is our attempt to synthesize our experience, learnings, and reflection in a way that will be useful in a practical way.

This is not a book to be read through and put down. It is a manual that can be used as a guide to ways of centering, to new forms of prayer. And it also offers scripture passages corresponding to each of the personality types.

The book is intended for all who seriously undertake the inner journey and seek a greater transparency before God. It is also intended for retreat and spiritual directors as an aid to their understanding of the world of their directees.

This book is not intended as a basic study of the Enneagram. It is expected that the reader will have participated in an Enneagram workshop prior to using the material in these pages and extended their knowledge by reading *The Enneagram: A Journey of Self Discovery* by Beesing, Nogosek and O'Leary.

CHAPTER ONE
A Case For The Enneagram

With the words, "It was the best of times and the worst of times," Charles Dickens described his experience and the age of nineteenth century England during the Industrial Revolution. These words aptly portray for us the two faces of our present world situation. Any commentator or observer of the current world could focus on particular aspects which mirror stark dimensions of goodness or evil. It is vital for us to begin this way as we have experienced the Enneagram Typology as making a positive contribution to persons and thus impacting the world as we know it.

On the one hand, it is "the best of times." Human ingenuity and creativity have created startling technological advances. These have changed our means of communication, travel and medical treatment, to mention but a few of the areas affected by scientific advances. In 1880, our ancestors in Boston would communicate by letter or telegraph, travel by rail or stage coach and undergo medical examination by sight and touch and some basic instruments. In 1987 we communicate by voice terminal around the world by telstar, travel by plane or automobile and have x-rays, scans, or other laboratory tests to determine our physical condition. Peoples have formed movements which have struggled for freedom from political or economic bondage, e.g., in the Phillipines or South Africa. In the United States and some other western countries this has a particular shape in the movement for equality among minority groups and the women's movement which seek personal, social, political, economic and sometimes religious freedom. In Latin America, small communities (base communities and Gospel reflection/action groups), have been sources of vitality for the Christian communities which have suffered from forms of repression. Blacks in South Africa have protested the unjust system of apartheid. Seeds of hope are found in the American Bishops' Conference Pastorals which have taken critical looks at both the perilous world situation of stalemate between nuclear powers in *The Challenge of Peace* and at the American and world economy in the light of the Gospel in the *Pastoral Letter on Catholic Social Teaching and the U.S. Economy.*

On the other hand, it is "the worst of times." On the global scene as we near the end of the twentieth century, division, not peace and unity, is the key descriptive word. There are the "haves" and the "have nots" as economic and military power reside in the Northern Hemisphere. Moreover, this part of the world controls 80% of the world's resources. A nuclear stand-off exists between the two super powers (USA and USSR) with only continuing ineffectual talking about arms limitations. On that score, the horizon is not promising, as the future may entail more nations able to join the nuclear club. Nationalism controls policies and actions of peoples around the globe. No international body could hold the USSR accountable for its slowness in disclosing the Chernobyl nuclear power plant accident, which was of vital concern to its neighbors, nor can any international agency prohibit the USA from aiding the contras against the Nicaraguan government, a policy which has met with the disapproval of many South and Central American countries. A detailed analysis of the causes of our present situation is obviously beyond the scope of our work. Yet few would dispute our pointing at excessive individualism, competitiveness and nationalism as prime causes of at least part of the global struggle we have focused on.

In the United States (and many other industrial nations) the marital convenant has suffered from an alarming divorce rate. Approximately one out of every two marriages ends in divorce. Even in the Catholic Church, long a supporter of marital covenant, the percentage of marital breakdown is near the national average. Moreover, since the 1960's, numerous priests and religious have left their way of life. In our society today, the value of a permanent commitment to any way of life is often put into question. Great economic pressure lays on the average family and in response to such demands households often have two spouses working. This results in the phenomenon of diminishing parental guidance and the so-called "latch key children." The drive for upward mobility places additional pressure on families as each generation can try to reproduce or outstrip their parents' condition. One of the unfortunate results is a loss in our society of some of the friendliness, beautiful relational qualities of family life, extended family ties which are still prevalent in many less developed areas of the world, such as Africa. Hunger and homelessness are stark realities at home and abroad. In the Catholic Church, as well as in other Christian bodies, there are great tensions about Church teaching and Church practice, e.g., a theologian is prohibited from teaching on a faculty of Theology, a bishop has his teaching role curtailed and ordination of women has led to a decrease of one third of the participants in the Episcopal Church.

Many different ways and paths are being taken to address our world situation. The problematic might be dealt with through psychology, economics, world politics, etc. Some of the approaches to solutions proceed from a view of the human person which is only partial and may leave out entirely the spiritual nature of humanity. Fragmented in that way, man or woman can be seen as a "consumer," "worker," "foreigner," (alien by virtue of race, creed, gender or nation). We stand within a tradition of Christian Spirituality. Our view is that spirituality encompasses the whole of human life, and is a response to the Spirit of God in life.

In the course of our years of ministry, we have become acquainted with the Enneagram which, like a sleeping giant, awakened in our times[1] and marched out of the shadows of obscurity. This understanding of the human personality was employed within the Moslem tradition by Sufi mystics with their disciples, although most likely not originated by them. Our own experience with it and its use in many spiritual centers in our country have shown its applicability in a general way to human persons and not something restricted to a certain group of people. We share the view of many persons that the personality typology is helpful in promoting God's vision of the human person and community.

The Judeo-Christian tradition views the human person as made in the image of God. Each person is unique, irreplaceable, gifted and struggling. Though endowed with gifts and talents, each person is also flawed by weakness and sinfulness. God's design for the individual in whom God delights is the "man or woman fully alive." Our compassionate God likewise has a plan of unity, peace and justice for the whole human family. The Lord's prayer (Mt. 6:9-13) viewed as a summary of God's intention and desire for us, proclaims God's love ordered towards the realization of the reign of justice, love, peace and truth in all its fullness.

Personal Level

As teachers of the Enneagram and spiritual directors, we have found it beneficial for people on the personal, interpersonal and social spheres of human existence. A basic question that a person faces in the human journey is that of identity, "Who am I?" Recent work in developmental psychology has reflected on that question as it emerges with different nuances at different stages of the human journey. Most of the persons with whom we work individually and in programs throughout the country are in their 30's and beyond. They have had life experience and often some counseling experience. However well they know themselves, there is always a deepening clarity which emerges when a person finds one's Enneagramic personality type. The awareness that dawns on persons is like a "light shining in one's closet." Indispensable for human and spiritual growth is self-knowledge.

The late Dag Hammarskjold, the former Secretary-General of the United Nations, perceptibly remarked that we have become adept at exploring outer space, but that we have not developed similar skills in exploring our own inner spaces. In fact, he wrote: "The longest journey is the journey inwards."[2] The true self that we are to discover is the image or word of God that each of us is uniquely, but which is hidden within the depths of the person. On the way of this journey we become aware not only of our conscious selves but also of the unconscious aspects of the self which are unknown, forgotten and beyond conscious control. The unconscious dimension of the personality needs healing and liberation as well for the self to become whole. Teilhard de Chardin in *The Divine Milieu* reflects on this in a striking passage:

We must try to penetrate our most secret self, and examine our being from all sides. Let us try, patiently, to perceive the ocean of forces to which we are subjected and in which our growth is, as it were steeped. . . . And so, for the first time in my life perhaps (although I am supposed to meditate every day!), I took the lamp and, leaving the zone of everyday occupations and relationships where everything seems clear, I went down into my inmost self, to the deep abyss whence I feel dimly that my power of action emanates. But as I moved further and further away from the conventional certainties by which social life is superficially illuminated, I became aware that I was losing contact with myself. At each step of the descent a new person was disclosed within me of whose name I was no longer sure, and who no longer obeyed me. And when I had to stop my exploration because the path faded from beneath my steps, I found a bottomless abyss at my feet. . . . And if someone saved me, it was hearing the voice of the Gospel . . . speaking to me from the depth of the night: *ego sum, noli timere* (It is I, be not afraid).[3]

As this passage reminds us, a key to self-understanding and spiritual growth is prayer. In genuine prayer a person moves from a more rational and wordy consciousness to a deeper and more intuitive awareness. Teilhard was reflecting on that experience. A widely accepted explanation of that movement is the so-called "filter theory."[4] In this theory, the brain and nervous system are fitted with restrictive filters or barriers of some kind which prevent total reality from entering consciousness, only permitting the entrance of such knowledge as a human being needs for survival. The filters screen reality for the human being and act as a repressive mechanism calculated to impede the entrance of knowledge that would otherwise overwhelm us. Thus the screen is protective, for humankind, unable to bear too much reality, has to find ways of blocking things out. These protective barriers can be removed, thus expanding the mind. The barriers can be lifted by drugs, perhaps break down in certain types of mental illness or are less restrictive in persons gifted with mental telepathy and clairvoyance. Prayer is also a human and natural way of opening the filters, welcoming the inflow of reality, and expanding the mind. Generally, the process is gradual, in daily prayer where the barriers are slowly lifted to allow an influx of greater reality into consciousness. Sometimes, however, the barriers are removed more rapidly, leading to great enlightenment.

As crucial as this self knowledge is, human persons employ many escapes (relationships, work, addictions, etc.) which prevent them from looking at the truth about themselves. There is something within us which resists the truth, as desirable as it is in theory to accept it. The Enneagram has helped people to know their personal giftedness and name the shape of their struggles and peculiar sinfulness. This understanding has been a catalyst for self acceptance, an at-homeness with one's own gifts and compulsions, light and darkness. New energies are released within the human person as they need no longer strive to be other than what they are. A healthy sense of humor about their own failings and sinfulness enables persons to hold the treasure that they are lightly and gently. In the persons' inner world they can now accept themselves as persons in process, rather than the defended image they previously presented of themselves. God works with us best when we are moist clay. St. Irenaeus put it succinctly: "It is not you that shape God, it is God that shapes you. If then you are the work of God, await the hand of the artist who does all things in due season. Offer him your heart, soft and tractable, and keep the form in which the artist has fashioned you. Let your clay be moist, lest you grow hard and lose the imprint of his fingers."

Interpersonal Level

Our age shows an interest in whatever fosters interpersonal relationships and community. There is a growing realization that we need to discover how to live together without destroying one another on this crowded planet. Hence, there have sprung up in recent years: new forms of community living, sensitivity training, group encounters, workshops on communication skills, etc. A further dimension of this is the modern focus on intimacy. Intimacy is generally acknowledged as a stage in the growth to human maturity and an expectation and requirement for marriage in our time. Intimacy involves an ability to disclose one's thoughts, feelings, plans and vision in an open and trusting way with others.

In interpersonal relationships there emerges as a result of self-knowledge and knowledge of others acquired through the Enneagram Personality Typology, when received and prayerfully reflected upon, a new appreciation and acceptance of others. A recurring experience with other persons when we measure them by ourselves is the sense: "I would not have thought, felt, or acted like that." Instead of a reverential looking at others our attitude can be a desire to fashion them in our peculiar image. In working with the Enneagram, people begin to see how different others really are. There are nine different Personality Types, masks, with their motivations and affective flavor that confront us in the persons of our world. People also discover the why of a common experience: some of these personalities are easier for me to understand and accept because of a natural flow of energy; others are difficult for me to accept because of an antipathy and affection which emerge.

The Enneagramic understanding of the human person is a help to live the great commandment of love because it calls us beyond a mere tolerance of the gifts and compulsiveness of others. As Christians we are challenged to become patient and compassionate with others whose struggle in life can be so different than our own. At other times, our new understanding of others can be generative in relationships, ministry or business. Our differences confront the expectation that each person can or should be able to do all things. Now we see the various gifts of the organizer, peace maker, idealist, visionary, etc. Such a perspective enables us to differentiate gifts and strengths and foster the unique capabilities of the persons whose lives we touch as friends, co-ministers or co-workers.

Social Sphere

In a 1985 report on American culture, *Habits of the Heart*,[5] Robert Bellah and associates traced the history of the fading American tradition of cooperation under the corrosive impact of another cultural

energy, individualism. This individualism had released many productive energies. But gone wild, it has
resulted in a corrupting greed, self seeking, and rejection of responsibility for community. This cultural
ethos stands in stark contrast both with our
biblical tradition and global interdependence. God's
revealed Word shows how He/She fashioned and
formed a people (Israel and Church). Indeed, God
chooses to save us only as we are linked and connected in life-giving and loving ways with one
another. Awareness of our global family has become
heightened in our time through communication
media, particularly through television. No people or
nation can be totally self-sufficient. Nations are in-
terdependent although our behavior does not
manifest this reality through just structures. We can
observe it certainly in the area of natural resources
which may be found in abundance in one area of the
globe, e.g., oil in the Near East, and our shirts or
dresses may wear a label from Taiwan or Korea. Yet
our connectedness is much more true at the spiritual
level; for male and female God made us, in God's image. The Enneagram Personality Typology discloses a
wealth of personalities which are like the brilliant colors which radiate from a multi-splendored diamond:
gold, blue, green, etc. The many sides enable the
brilliant reflections. So too, in the human family we
have a need to recognize and reverence the giftedness
of others, to foster the growth and wholeness of each
of the personalities. Otherwise, God's image will not
shine as clearly in our world. Individualism and com-
petition will be what stamps our approaches to other
persons and nations. We will continue to suffer with

and putting themselves in God's place. All Evil stems from these kinds of motivations and behavior, including (God forbid it happening) nuclear war. What is needed, then, is a change of mind, a change of heart—a radical conversion to God issuing in a loving and compassionate heart, a heart whose scope becomes more and more expansive, embracing all persons and influencing all persons by a generative love. For the Christian it is the Servant Jesus who lived this vocation to its fullness, becoming the Savior of all. He took on in his Passion and Death the woes of the world and suffered in love for humanity and the universe. And each person who grows to love all persons with a universal love, rejoices with those who rejoice and weeps with those who weep, has their own part in this redemptive process. Such was true of the apostle Paul ("Even now I find my joy in the suffering I endure for you. In my own flesh I fill up what is lacking in the sufferings of Christ for the sake of his body, the church." Col. 1, 24) or Pope John XXIII or Gandhi.[6] Love is the most powerful spiritual force in the universe.

Spirituality of the Enneagram

In this work we intend to focus on the spirituality of the Enneagram, particularly on Enneagram prayer. The reader can turn to other works which describe more extensively the Enneagram Personality Typology. It is not necessary here to reproduce those descriptions. However, the reader will need that basic knowledge to follow our reflections. Now in a summary fashion we will make a few points about the Enneagramic view of personality, the centers and nine personality types.

The Enneagramic view of personality postulates that each person is born with a purity of essence. One remains in that state for a short time. As a child immediately relates to the world around it and significant others who are the crucial influences for him or her, he/she finds himself/herself in need of defense against a world that is perceived as hostile. So the child develops a particular compulsive, defensive approach to life depending on the kind of energy that typifies the personality. Each person is born with a propensity, a preoccupation with a certain kind of energy. Somewhere in the first six years, perhaps between four and six, the child fashions a mask or an idealization in order to present the self and defend the self against the outside world. Every person develops a compulsive style of coping with the world. The styles are the nine personality types. The little girl or boy adopts one of these and remains that type, retains that basic life strategy during the course of his/her life. However, a person can be more or less compulsed as it is possible for the human person to become enlightened, face and work with the particular compulsive style one has adopted. An image of this is provided by the degrees on a thermometer. So one can meet a very compulsed perfectionist (a number ONE who exhibited the characteristics of this type from a 20 degree level of the thermometer. One can also meet the same personality type who at 80 degrees on the thermometer manifested much of the giftedness of the personality. The person of 80 degrees, who is enlightened, is the freer and healthier person.

Enlightenment often occurs for an individual in the course of conscious contact with one's loving and compassionate God. Before we treat prayer we need to expand our remarks on the Enneagram Centers of energy out of which these personality types operate.

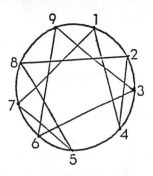

CHAPTER TWO
Characteristics of Enneagram Centers of Energy

Many persons who have struggled through layers of learned behavior and confusing relational patterns to find their Enneagram numbers have, in near despair, often asked, "Why is there not a tool similar to that used in the Meyers-Briggs personality inventory for finding one's Enneagram number?" Such a tool would make the work and time needed to situate oneself accurately in the system so much easier. Some presentors and writers of Enneagram theory have indeed used simple sets of questions to help persons in the search. The value of such an approach is at best quite limited. The questions touch behavior, not motivation.

A sample question posed might be, "Do you help others?" Two persons could be helpers, but for very different reasons. A number TWO whose idealization is, "I am helpful," helps because one is only good if one helps. A number SEVEN might also be helpful. The number SEVEN'S idealization is, "I am fine or O.K." The number SEVEN knows it is easier for people to be nice to one who is good to them. They help to avoid the pain that comes from negative responses such as anger directed toward them for not responding to need.

Many of the objective questions used in lists

seeking to lead people to claim a number need to be pushed to the level of motivation in order to test their validity to do what they are used to doing, namely, situate a person on the Enneagram circle.

Knowing that most students of the Enneagram theory have been exposed to descriptions about centers and personality types, we have chosen another approach in this chapter that may be helpful to the reader. It employs the use of imagery. Images often evoke greater depths in the human person than simple facts. We will talk about three cities. It is suggested that in reading the descriptives of the three cities that the reader try to reside within each city in turn. It would be important to reflect carefully upon one's experience. How did you feel? What was comfortable and right for you? What annoyed you? What would you like to change? Why? If you note certain mixed reactions and find yourself attracted to aspects of two centers, you might want to consider the possibility that the theory of the wings is involved.

This approach, hopefully, will be both enlightening and interesting for the reader.

It is not uncommon for us to hear described, or even ourselves, to describe a major city by means of a few carefully chosen adjectives. Some examples might read: New York is loud and successful; Boston, cultured and aristocratic; Philadelphia, respectable; Miami, opulent and recreational; Paris, sophisticated and fun-loving; Munich, hearty and lively. Such designations are an acknowledgment of very real differences in these cities in spite of their many common elements. The same naming or describing dynamic is often at work when we speak of people. There is a tendency often to think of one another in terms of the emotional tone of one's personality. One is controlled, another creative, still another lazy. The emotional tones of personality we perceive in our interactions with one another are, in fact, simply the outer expression of the person's inner world or inner city.

To retrieve our descriptions of the three specific types of energy in the Enneagram Personality study from the barrenness of factual naming of characteristics, we have chosen an entry into each center using three images of inner cities, each unique and each revealing quite starkly the characteristics of the particular center described. It is our hope that the images employed will move the reader to more than just an intellectual assent to particular characteristics of a center or a personality type, but rather into a feeling for the experience of living within the reality of that center or number.

The Head Centered City

Flying over *Caput,* one is immediately struck by the meticulous outlay of the city. The streets are ordered in parallel rows, the parks strategically placed and the buildings for community functions easily accessible from most points within the city limits. One notes also in making the landing approach to the city in the late night hours that the streets are uniformly and perfectly lighted. Entering the city itself from its small, but functional airport, one is struck by the manner of naming the streets. For parallel streets in one direction, numbers are used. The streets that intersect these streets at right angles are named by letters followed by names of persons continuing the alphabetical motif. Road signs are bright, clear and patterned. Careful, logical, functional planning is evidenced everywhere.

The homes of the dwellers of *Caput* are for the most part simple and unpretentious, although some are quite modern, a few quite adventuresome in design and many with solar heating. A feature that seems quite remarkable is that many of the homes have a kind of glass in their large picture windows which makes seeing out possible, but does not allow the pedestrian to view what is going on within. Fences with locked gates surround many of the homes while security guards are in evidence near public buildings. The streets are remarkably quiet and deserted.

As one passes several large colleges, universities and research centers in close proximity to one another, it becomes obvious that *Caput* is a center of learning. Modern, extensive libraries also strike the visitor. The overall tone of the city is one of patterned planning and reserve rather than spontaneity and splash.

The persons who dwell in *Caput* are the head centered Enneagram personalities; personalities concerned with practicality, logic and fitting in. A basic stance of giving ground rather than holding it and a rejection of aggression by the people in this center creates an atmosphere of non-violence and gentleness. Because these people find themselves living often in their own inner world of thoughts, ideas and plans, it is difficult for them to express openly their depth of feeling. A sense of cordiality and friendliness characterizes interactions, rather than genuine warmth and spontaneity. With fear as the least controlled emotion in this center, lighting, guarding and care are always in evidence.

The central church of *Caput* is St. Thomas, the Apostle. A remarkable feature of the church is its beautiful stained glass window depicting Thomas' recognition of Jesus after the resurrection, a scene which in some ways captures the spirit of the church. It is simple, stark, reverent, logically laid out. It speaks of the fact that "Seeing is believing."

Style does not seem to be a major issue among the dwellers of *Caput*. One would note an almost universal lack of sophistication in dress although some of the persons have a remarkable sense of color. Perhaps the word "childlike" would be a good description for the way the people present themselves.

Staying with the dwellers of *Caput*, one gets a real sense of being carefully observed and watched rather than attentively listened to. When a person of this city is invited to visit outside the city limits, one is always struck by the detailed directions that are sought before making the journey.

Everyone in *Caput* was not like everyone else. We observed three types of people there. Once at an office party a very reserved man in a plain suit stood within a circle which was reflecting on current issues. He took no part but seemed to be taking it all in. We thought he felt that he had nothing to contribute. He gave us an impression of being uncomfortable in the gathering. Much time went by and his reticence continued. His employer, who had invited us, had extolled his wisdom, but we were seeing none of this. The topic of conversation changed to the poetry of Emily Dickinson. Still our silent man made no effort to engage in it. His colleagues invited him to share some of his thoughts with us. To our amazement he began to speak at length and knowledgeably about this topic of lifetime interest and study for him. This man would be described as number FIVE who idealizes the self as "I am wise."

Our second evening in *Caput* found us accepting from a woman an invitation to dinner at her home. On our arrival we were immediately struck by her warmth and graciousness. Within a short time we felt right at home. The woman had three daughters about whom she obviously liked to talk. Her conversation exhibited a worry and fear about the course of some of the events of their lives. We had the impression of someone who walked with a lot of fear. At one point we began to speak about the national government which had just invaded the tiny state of Grenada. Our listener was paralyzed by the critical questions and comments that were registered. She could not seem to entertain the possibility of thinking apart from the leader's decision and actions. We would type our hostess as a number SIX who idealized the self: "I am faithful;" "I am loyal."

We were at the civic center on our final day as people were having a celebration in honor of the police chief. There we met a woman who stood out from the others because of her bright clothing and lively personality. She had a very cheery countenance.

Her enthusiasm was catchy as she told of her plans for her next vacation. The way she described it, everything would be beautiful. One of us remarked afterwards that there seemed to be "no flat tires" in her life. Once the conversation touched on a heavy issue of replacing the head of the school committee. It became heated and before we knew what had happened the cheery woman had changed the topic of conversation. Somehow she had once again introduced some humor and was holding forth with her positive and optimistic viewpoints. There seemed to be no place for pain in her life. Everything was bouncy and light. This type of person, a number SEVEN on the Enneagram, idealized the self as "I am fine;" "I am O.K."

The days at *Caput* were quiet and reflective ones, but also marked by a stretching into the realm of possibilities and often doing that in a spirit of lightness and joy.

The Heart Centered City

The city of *Cordis,* located less than a hundred miles from *Caput*, both in its external layout and inner values seemed light years away from *Caput*. It is a city obviously built without a plan. One might say a seed of new housing was planted wherever there were relationships or human needs. The houses were close together, people talked with great regularity from porch to porch or over fences, and well-worn paths ran between homes. Shades were seldom drawn.

As logic and practicality seemed to dominate *Caput*, relationships, sociability and status dominated *Cordis*. People were warm, friendly and demonstrative in their affection.

The newcomer would be immediately struck by the number of uniformed nurses and social workers walking the streets in route to or from work. Many, many people seemed to be in the helping professions. Numerous hospitals, clinics and service agencies were located in this city.

Image was unquestionably an important issue to the *Cordis* dweller. Many of the people wore, with great comfortability, the latest styles. People jogged, weight loss clinics were numerous, and conversation often centered around weight, style and accomplishment.

Political candidates were promoted by means of large signs adorning the flowered gardens of many homes. Honor rolls remembering achievements of many kinds were in public squares. Nailed to trees and on the community bulletin boards were signs announcing up-coming square dances, rallies and occasionally a fun time such as a pie eating contest. There were numerous theaters and movie houses. Clubs such as Boy and Girl Scouts, Knights of Columbus and women's clubs, etc., were numerous and portrayed by their ads.

The Church of St. Martha in *Cordis* was rather startling to enter. Banners adorned the walls; pews had been removed and replaced by pillows. In passing the church, one would often hear strains of singing that evidenced the strong charismatic climate of the prayer and liturgical worship.

The city of *Cordis* was strongly reflective of the

relational quality of the heart center. Vitality, image and social concern impacted the visitor from the moment of arrival.

At *Cordis* we met three other personality types when we attended our annual convention. The chairperson invited us to be guests for tea at her home. She showed a constant concern in her activity while we were there to make us happy and attend to our every need. A number of phone calls punctuated our visit. Apparently, people counted on her to help in different needs and projects. Once she let her exasperation show with the remark: "You would think that they could get someone else to do that. Why do I always have to do everything?" Our hostess was constantly up and down from the table and seemed unable to simply sit with us and relax. As we reflected later on our conversation, it became apparent that she had acquired a great deal of information and knowledge about us, but we had heard her say very little about herself. She seemed to want to be a very independent person and not acknowledge that she, too, had needs. This was our first contact with a number TWO personality who idealizes the self as "I am helpful;" "I can give." We were to meet many more in this city.

Cordis is the locale of one of our offices. While we were there, we had an appointment with our local district manager. Her secretary ushered us in to meet her. Her office immediately struck us as totally equipped with the latest model in computer terminals, copier machines, inter-office voice terminals, etc. Charts and goals covered the walls. She was dressed smartly in a business suit and met us at the appointed time. After a couple of polite words we launched immediately into business issues. We had come to see her because the *Cordis* branch was below its previous performance. She alleged all sorts of reasons to explain it, was confident that it was only a temporary slow down, and assured us that nothing she had done had contributed to the present turndown of production. We found her quite defensive in this and vigorous in presenting her own successful image. Our files had told us about her. She had moved quickly up the ranks of the company and always wanted to be where the action was. We remarked to one another after the appointment that she seemed impersonal in her contact with us. She had been friendly, very articulate and functionally professional. We know her as the number THREE personality who idealizes the self as "I am successful;" "I am efficient." We met many others in the managerial section of the company in this city.

Before we left *Cordis* we had a dinner engagement with an old friend. He was single and invited us to his condominium. As we entered his apartment, we were struck with the quiet elegance of the living room. Several paintings and statues added a special tone to the room. Quiet, reflective music accompanied our conversation and meal. He had prepared a dinner for us and the arrangements of the colors of the food accentuated our gourmet treat. That evening we became involved in nostalgia. As we talked of the past, we became aware of the depth of mourning and loss that he expressed about some of the events of his life. The dramatization of events was increased by his frequent use of images and symbols. At times, a touch of affectation entered his speech. He gave his remembrances in vivid and picturesque language. For him nothing was simple and ordinary. We commented on his excellent physical condition. He attributed it to his diet and exercise and showed us his brand new stylish jogging outfit. Before we left *Cordis* he insisted that we take his box at the theatre, as an excellent play had come that week to the city. We describe our friend as a number FOUR personality who idealizes the self as "I am special;" "I am sensitive;" "I am refined."

Time spent in *Cordis* was a social time, a time seldom, if ever, spent alone. One left *Cordis* happy to have shared life with the persons dwelling there, but somehow knowing the need for time and space to enter into the deeper world of silence and reflection.

The Gut Centered City

Humus was the third city we visited. Its distinctiveness was equally as marked as that of *Caput* or *Cordis*. This city was one which preserved a strong sense of history and tradition. A touch of the past was immediately visible. Museums abounded. Houses were not new and would impress the visitor as being more functional than aesthetic or artistic. There was much uncultivated land. Vegetable gardens, rather than flower gardens, dominated the landscape. The people of *Humus* seemed relatively unconcerned about style. Their dress was unpretentious in style and color, without the adornment of either jewels or makeup. One would say the people of Humus—men, women and children—lived close to the earth. Their eating habits were still further indication of the simplicity of their lives and interests. Health foods were sold, camping grounds and woods were the popular places of recreation and vacation.

The *Humus* dwellers were deeply concerned with issues of justice and the environment. It was not uncommon to see demonstrators marching or standing on street corners to openly express their concerns for their issues.

The city was noisy, even boisterous at times. The people were back-slappers, comfortably confrontative and argumentative. A sense of real spontaneity in encounters and an obvious lack of polish in speech and self-expression was immediately evident. One was invariably struck with the simplicity and honesty of the people. Image was not highly valued.

The city never seemed to stop. Night and day the sounds of the city would waft their way into the consciousness of the visitor. St. Peter's Church was the place of worship for the Catholics of *Humus*. A burlap banner of Peter jumping in the water to reach the resurrected Jesus was the dominant visual to greet the worshipper. Fishing nets draped on the walls of the church completed the rustic sea motif. There was an obvious interface between spirituality and the justice issues in this parish. One needed only to listen to the homilies preached or the concern expressed in the prayer of the faithful. Food collections were frequent for the hungry and marginalized. Issues of global and local need were kept before the worshipper on the several bulletin boards in the church. The spirituality was earthy and rooted in human life.

Sports were a value to the people of *Humus*. The competitive nature of the most popular sports reflected the spirit of the people. *Humus* prided itself on its championship football, hockey and wrestling teams.

In *Humus* we met three other personality types. We responded to an invitation from an acquaintance to play golf at the *Humus* City Links. Our host was a powerful man who seemed to delight in controlling things and in making others uncomfortable. He got into a shouting match with the golf party ahead of us whom he claimed was playing too slowly. The language he used was crude and cutting. When we seemed surprised, he told us that he always got what he deserved. Once he said that he had complained loudly and boisterously to the manager of a supermarket because he had found only one pecan in a gallon of butter pecan ice cream. He got a new half gallon. Among his interests were many causes and volunteer service in the neighborhood tennis association. He gave us the sense that he had the power to change things. He encouraged us not to be weak in expressing our needs or complaints. He let us know his difficulty in dealing with any sort of weakness. This man was a number EIGHT personality who idealized the self as "I am powerful;" "I am strong."

In our golf party that day was a friend of our number EIGHT personality. This woman appeared as a model of peacefulness. She was the one affected most by the shouting. She tried immediately to calm down her friend when he got into the argument. We heard her try to pacify the other party by telling them what a hard day he had had. It seemed she would go to all lengths to have things settled down. She seemed easily satisfied with her life and had no driving sense of purpose. She told us how she collected various things, stored tooth brushes because she had found a kind she liked and had six of her favorite raisin cakes in her office desk so that she would not have the hassle of trying to find them again. In fact, we conjectured that a lot of this woman's energy went into resting, settling others down and trying to remain undisturbed. She was a number NINE who idealized the self as "I am set;" "I am settled."

We were in *Humus* at election time. Our number EIGHT acquaintance suggested that we must attend a political rally to get another flavor of the city. It was a loud and boisterous evening. We made acquaintance there with an idealistic young man. His view of the present city government was very critical. He seemed to have some ideal measure with which he took apart the present leadership. He used his rapier-like wit to find flaws and faults in almost everything. No one was spared, including himself. He spoke with an edge in his voice and gave the impression that he did not know how angry he actually was. This man is our number ONE personality who idealizes the self as "I am right;" "I am correct."

One left *Humus* feeling refreshed, challenged and in touch again with human life in the raw. It almost seemed difficult to re-enter a world of sophistication and pretense, of ideas and plans after such starkness and simplicity of life in *Humus*.

As you visited each of the three cities, where did you feel most comfortable? Where would you like to live? Did you find yourself remarkably like any of the persons living in that city?

TEACH ME YOUR WAYS, O LORD

Prayer

Have you ever read or heard the statement, "Prayer is the simplest thing out," and found yourself not even giving reflective space within yourself to the statement because of the years of struggle that have marked your own earnest efforts to commune with God? Has a retreat director ever suggested that you get directly angry with God and, in the suggesting, hinted at the fact that expressing your anger to God would open the gates to palaces of peace within you, only to find yourself totally unable to experience God as the object of your anger? Has the enthusiasm and joy of a genuine charismatic left

you with a tinge of envy at the treasures that had been
opened for them, and yet feeling so uncomfortable in
your own efforts at charismatic prayer? Have you
ever turned to centering prayer as a place, at last, to
touch God in your own core and found yourself able
to do nothing more than sleep? It is our experience
that one or several of the descriptives above fit all persons who have seriously entered into a life of prayer.
In spite of that fact, we would still affirm our opening
statement that, "Prayer is the simplest thing out."

Prayer is presence to the presence of God. Our
prayer is also unique to each of us. Without question
the personalities described in Chapter 2 of this work
are extremely individual in their way of being with
themselves, their world and also their God. To pray,
we must come before God not only as we are, but also
with an awareness of the ways in which we find it
possible to center, to move in faith from the outer
world of images and thoughts to the world of faith
and gift. The shapes of our struggles to face God are
as unique as we are unique. Among the many books
written on prayer, there is scarcely any mention of the
particular difficulties people might have entering into
communication with God. As we begin some basic
reflections on prayer, we would like to share some
preliminary thoughts on the topic and suggest some
universal conditions without which there can be no
prayer life that will be genuine or sustained.

Prayer must become a value if I am ever to learn
to pray. There are few of us who would be unwilling
to claim with great honesty that prayer is a value, but
do we ever make a distinction in our own minds between values and value indicators? My values are those

things I consistently choose from among alternates. Daily schedules include many things: work, eating, exercising, friends, etc. Do I consistently choose to pray when I could do something else? Only if my answer is yes to that question can I say prayer is a value for me. A second important truth to remember in learning to pray is that I learn to pray by praying. A tennis player learns about the game by reading books about tennis but only becomes a skilled player by getting onto the court and entering into the sport itself. We learn about prayer from books. We learn to pray by praying.

We need to come as we are to this act of worship and love which we call prayer. We need to come to know our real selves and to be able to be relaxed and free with our God. Many of us hide from God in prayer. The reason for this can be the ways we've internalized our reading about prayer. We can find ourselves trying to be quiet, reverent, centered when we haven't acknowledged that as we enter into the posture of prayer we are, in fact, none of what we are trying to be. We might in fact be angry, excited, disappointed, tender, or hurt at the time we choose to pray. We are invited by God to come as we are.

Who is this God who has created me with a capacity to commune with Him/Her and desires intensely that I come as I am? Our images of God must constantly be expanded by an ever deeper knowledge of the face of the Divine reflected in Jesus. He is one who goes about doing good, who eats with sinners, who can be gentle and forgiving in some of the areas of human life that we have been formed to be most judgmental e.g., sins of the flesh. He stands in stern condemnation of some of the more respectable sins of human life that pass unnoticed, e.g., righteousness. This is the God before whom we stand in prayer.

We can learn a great deal about our ways of being before God from our reflective awareness of our interpersonal relationships. We relate to God as we relate to others. Perhaps reflection on our relationships of love and friendship could practically open the door to a more relaxed presence to God. We could say we pray to each other in our exchanges with those we love or trust. Reflect upon how you are with a friend. Do you recognize the same approach to a friend as the way you relate to God? Are you free and spontaneous with the former and guarded and standing on ceremony with the latter? At what level of communication do you feel trusting enough to share with a friend, e.g., daily events, personal feelings, ideas, vision or spiritual experiences? We do influence each other. We all know the experience of becoming angry at another, experiencing a gentling of our spirit, or being challenged or affirmed by another. There is no prayer unless we allow the Lord to be active, vibrant and initiating in our lives. Prayer can never remain simply the deciding of our solutions to life's problems and the effort to convince God to see the wisdom of our ways.

It takes a great deal of trust to pray. Prayer involves for all of us who have entered seriously into it an Abrahamic experience, an ability to move from what is known to what is unknown. The person who prays will be different from the non-prayer. Prayer is not an achievement. It is not a question of analyzing one's stage of prayer. It is rather standing openly and lovingly before One by whom we know we are loved in increasing unselfconsciousness. It is a willingness to be unmasked, unprotected and transparent. It is a recognition of how much God desires us to stand before Him/Her so that He/She can love us. As in all moments and experiences of love, receptivity is genuinely important and integral, so also in a life of prayer.

One's prayer can never be compared to or judged by other's any more than one's way of approaching a friend can become normative for another. One's prayer, if it is real, will be as unique as the person praying is unique. It will grow as we grow and will come to renounce once and for all the desire to return to prayer styles and forms of early life just to reclaim good feeling, knowing that we are different and loved in our new stages of development by a God who walks tenderly with us.

Prayer, in spite of all that has been said, is not purely a personal reality. Our best gift to the world is our own experience of God. The human spirit is anguishing from an often unnamed hunger, the hunger for the face of God. The man or woman of prayer intrudes into society and societal values an experience of God, an intrusion vital to the survival of the human spirit.

The Enneagram study can be a tremendous help in our personal lives of prayer. It is a gift that clearly names for us our masks or protective stances before one another which become for us our ways of hiding from God. The Enneagram specifies for us the energies that are preferred in us and makes it possible for us to learn styles and ways of prayer that are natural and comfortable—prayer styles that seem tailor made for us. The Enneagram study can lead us to a real comfortability with what is best for us in such a way that dabbling in a variety of forms is no longer necessary. Respect for others' ways of approaching God grows rather than the competitive stances that can lead us to a debunking or comparative putting down of ways that are not comfortable for us. Ways of being with the Word of God and the Word of Life can be learned for each energy center and each personality type.

Conversion: The Fruit of Prayer

When we pray, we respond to the invitation to come close to God, to stand in God's light. In that light we come to see ourselves, others and the world from God's viewpoint. This coming close and new vision has serious implications for our personal, interpersonal and social lives. What we see, if we are willing to brave the light, penetrates deeply into the core of our beings. A crisis of meaning is precipitated. What is the meaning of my life? Of life itself?

In the face of such questions, past values, loyalties, and ways of being offer no help. We find ourselves unmasked, with so much of what was previously meaningful becoming relative. The moments of greatest communion with God are often accompanied by an experience of terrible newness. This newness, if assented to, we begin to realize, has the power to destroy what is inauthentic within us:—the darkness, the unfreedoms and the unreflected postures.

The experience of God in prayer moves us into the context of our own human stories where we can respond in the concrete to our new vision and the deeper calls of God.[1] It is in our personal history that we see clearly values that we have and live by. Adopted and often unreflected attitudes also come clear. When we have stood in an unprotected way in God's light, we find our way of being marked by the awareness that characterizes a traveler in a new land. We have a heightened sense of the realities of our lives. We begin to be able to name who we really are and who we are not; our limits, traps, affections, falseness and unfreedoms come clear as do our beautiful gifts.

This new and heightened awareness carries with it invitations. These basically are invitations to a more and more reflective stance toward life. We come to realize that genuine conversion will come in the stuff of ordinary experiences and human relationships. There is need to listen to these experiences, to our suffering, to desires and to life itself. It is only when our experiences are reflected that they will penetrate our depths. The real crisis of meaning will be faced by reflection that is sustained in our life and interior affective response to life. Many answers and much meaning will be found within. From within us begin the new shoots of greater health and fullness of life.

Implicit in turning to the light of truth and awareness is the corresponding call to turn from the darkness, the inauthentic. The inauthentic has many faces: that which is not lived, that which is unfree, that which is unloving, to mention a few.

All that leads us to recognize the truth of ourselves and leads us to choose the light over the darkness. Our images, our dreams, our affections, our choices can be among our greatest sources of light. It is by this growing and expanded awareness that we can come to new ways of caring, loving, and listening and move toward the abandonment of a life that is incomplete.

The invitations that prayer extends can be frightening. We are invited to go where we have not been before, to abandon the supports with which we have traveled the previous journeys of our lives. We don't know what we will find. We do know somehow, however vaguely, that there will be some measure of ego loss. All is terribly frightening and at the same time terribly compelling. It is only with the confidence in a loving God journeying with us that anyone would have the courage to undertake the interior journey with any seriousness. The experience of God's love is the core spiritual experience without which there can be very little real spiritual growth or freedom.[2]

Where does all of this fit in with the Enneagram study? We all know the experience of having a needle stick on a record and the constant repetition of just one groove of the record. We suffer the limitation when we know the beauty of the whole record and are only able to experience a small part because of the crack in the record. We also know what it would be like to be locked in a room with the possibility of seeing our town from only one window. We would know the limitation and yearn for more.

Each of us, in our Enneagram number, has our

groove, our locked room. We have become familiar with hearing and seeing one aspect of reality in the form of our idealization over and over again with the result that we lose the total picture of reality and its beauty. We hear such grooves as: I am good because I am successful (THREE); I am good because I am faithful (SIX); or I am good because I am wise (FIVE).

From our window in our locked room, our life view is limited. We might see only what is imperfect in life (ONE). We might consistently experience the world as unjust and only see people oppressing one another (EIGHT). Our only view of life may be to look on the world as aching need (TWO).

Without the flash of light, so like the lightning illuminating the darkened landscape on a summer night, we never see reality clearly. Without the flash of lightning we might only wonder what an unfamiliar landscape holds. Without the flashes of God's light with which we are gifted in prayer, we continue to grope in fear and insecurity. We do not hear parts of the record of life that bring us to wholeness, nor do we see life in a way that we know the possibilities of acting more freely.

The continued limitation of our view of life creates in each of us a certain emotional tone that in honest self awareness we come to name. We can be gluttonous for the good things of life (SEVEN); envious of others (FOUR); or slothful (NINE). In the light we come to know what in particular each of us needs to struggle with, what virtues we need to acquire to counteract the limitations of our particular personality.

Prayer is being with a God who loves us uncondi-
tionally, and responds to our need, and not just as we
deserve. He/She journeys with us as we venture into
the lands of freedom that the flashes of God's gifting
let us glimpse.

How best, given who each of us is, can we be
with our God in a sustained and loving way?
Hopefully, the chapters that follow will speak to that
question.

Centering

So much has been written these last years on the
topic of centering. In Christian spirituality we have
come to listen reverently to the wisdom of the East,
and at the same time hold generously open to the East
the treasury of our spiritual tradition. In the chapters
that follow, we will delve deeply into our own lavish
tradition, but also savor the gift of Eastern spirituality that will aid our presentations and understanding.

When we think of centering, it is important to
acknowledge the state we often find ourselves in as we
come to prayer. It is the state in which we experience
life. We do not hear the music of life. It is a
background of which we are unaware. We do not see
the stars because there is so much brightness and at-
traction in the complexity of our daily living. We do
not smell the flowers. There simply isn't time. We do
not touch our own center. We are, by the pace of life,
hurried on to the next experience before we can go
deeply into our feeling and being.

An image we might use for ourselves when we
come to prayer is that of an airplane arriving at the

terminal. Our motors are still running, we are crowded with people, busy with ideas and plans, and often
controlled by hopes and fears.

What are we seeking in entering into the experience of centering? What is the goal of centering?
Basically, we might say we seek an ability to attend to
what is deeper, an ability to dwell upon the reality of
God. We seek an ability to exclude what is irrelevant
and superficial and open ourselves to the relevant
truth of things and attend to a development of a
presence.

We have been given aids and techniques to reach
this deeper awareness. Most of us are familiar with
some of these such as just sitting, use of the mandala
or mantra. Basically, there are three particular ways
of coming to the center and each has a particular
usefulness for the centers of the Enneagram. Before
we describe the different ways of centering, we need
to elaborate further on the centers themselves and
God's way with each of them.

A look at the Enneagram centers: Their inner and
outer worlds and their experiences of God.

Head Center

The head centered people of the Enneagram,
numbers FIVE, SIX, SEVEN, are the "Peeping
Toms" of the human family. They have a large inner
world and a small outer world. From their hiding
place, they tend to view reality without engaging in it.
Their difficulty is with being in the world. There is a
lot going on inside and they must often struggle to get
it outside. The inner world of the head centered per-

son is one of thoughts, plans, dreams and also fear.
They often experience strong feelings, but even these
feelings they have a hard time getting outside of
themselves. Others can experience them as lacking in
genuine emotion. Their ego is practical and they are
much more comfortable with doing than with talking
about doing. Most often God is experienced by the
head centered person in the outer realm. They will be
at home with concepts of God as friend, lover, companion, or master. Their most natural experience will
not lead them immediately to the experience of indwelling. They will know this in faith, but in prayer
there will be a spontaneous turning to God as outside
of themselves. This seems strange, considering the
large inner world in which they frequently live. What
is happening is that God is bringing about a harmony
between the inner and outer world by calling them
outside to meet God's self. We will often witness
these persons praying with their eyes open and
naturally choosing to light a candle.

Heart Center

The heart centered persons (TWO, THREE,
FOUR) are often referred to as the"fish in the bowl"
personalities of the Enneagram. They experience a
very large outer world and a small inner world. They
are constantly being pulled out of themselves by the
world around them and being invited to engage in it.
They always experience themselves as being seen by
others whose approval is vital to them. They are often
putty in the hands of others. The fact that it is hard
for these persons to forget that they are being looked

at keeps them in an almost constant state of anxiety.
Their lack of in-touchness with themselves often
makes their expression of feeling seem to lack the
quality of genuineness. Their deepest concerns are
with making connections with others and being approved of by them. The image ego controls in this
center.

God reveals Him/Herself to the heart centered
person as dwelling within. There is in this experience
an invitation to move within to the seldom dwelled in
mansions of their own lives and experiences. God
wishes to preside over their feelings, their thoughts,
their ways of loving and serving. Again God's gift
through prayer is to bring about a harmony in the
heart centered person between their inner world and
the outer world of their activity.

Gut Center

The "ship on the waves" is a good description of
the gut centered persons of the Enneagram, the
EIGHT, NINE, ONE personalities. These persons
have an equally developed inner and outer world in
which they alternately live. They move from one to
the other quite instinctively. Their energy is intense
and quick. They would know so well the experience
of St. Paul in Romans 7:14-25. In their inmost heart
they dearly love God's law and yet there is another
law they follow. They know the failure of frequent
resolutions broken and the power of the immediate in
their lives in spite of many good intentions. Anger,
therefore, is no stranger to them. For them there can
be a way of living within themselves and a very dif-

ferent way of being in the world. There is an instinctual disconnection between their inner and outer worlds. With their historical ego they often ask how things were in the past in making a decision and find themselves yet again out of touch with their own inner selves.

The gut centered person will experience God both within and without. For them, somehow, this communication of the divine will be their way of coming to connect the inner and outer realities of their worlds. They will experience God as friend, lover, companion, or master and, at the same time, know the experience of the indwelling. Relationship with both these ways of prayer will be comfortable for them. At a time of grace, when faced with the instinctual movement in the outer world, the EIGHT, NINE, ONE will recognize the God of their hearts and respond to the divine in the outer world. It is then that the connection is evident in their lives.

CHAPTER FOUR
Head Centered Prayer: Focused Meditation

Head centered people (FIVE, SIX, SEVEN) approach life in the manner of a violinist listening attentively to an orchestra for the correct measure and tempo of the music before beginning to play. They stand with their bows poised above the strings of life, and only when they know exactly how and when to join in, do they move freely and creatively. Feeling connected and at one with a situation are very important to the numbers FIVE, SIX, SEVEN. There is much about situating themselves, about being logical, and about knowing how pieces fit together that are part of their dynamic. Their connections with life are made through their sight and insight.

It would not be at all unusual in a group to meet the eyes of a head centered person. They tend to look around as a way of fitting themselves into a situation. Neither would it be unusual for one of them interiorly to look down the road at the possible developments of a proposed plan and suggest long term outcomes of decisions taken in the now.

They struggle to be in the world. Reality for them needs to be adjusted to. These persons have a very difficult time accepting both aggression and affection. They are guarded and do not want the environs of their lives to be infringed upon. After taking such care to fit into life, it would be again difficult for them to know how to act if their world had become altered or changed too quickly. Because of their own need to know where they are and what is expected of them there, they find it hard to disturb others or to hold their ground when an argument begins. They, as all of us, tend to think of others' approach to life as being similar to their own and do not want to be disruptive.

The head centered person is often guarded not only in expressing affection, but also in receiving it. Warmth and spontaneity are noticeably lacking in their affective expressions of themselves. They need time to adjust to others' advances and to assess logically the meaning and appropriateness of those advances as well as how they fit with the rest of life. Although their feelings can be quite well developed, these persons can appear to be extremely reserved and sometimes unaffectionate. This reserve is all part of their needing time and space to position themselves comfortably in reality and to remain in syntony (harmony) with their environment.

Sometimes persons might wonder how, in one situation, a personality such as number SEVEN could be the life of a party and at another time be quite shy and reticent. This observable phenomenon is all part of the positioning technique inherent in the head centered persons. In the former situation, the person was comfortable and connected and in the latter not yet feeling connected.

In the realm of dress or style the same dynamic is operative. The head centered persons seem to lack sophistication. It often takes them a bit longer than others to connect with the most recent changes in style. Seldom do they appear "mod," nor are they among the first to adopt a new style.

They can, because of their stance of observing life from the sidelines, even for a short space of time, appear more childlike than the other centers. We frequently experience them as taking time and sometimes as not quite sure how to act or speak.

Fear is the emotion least controlled in this center. The numbers FIVE, SIX, SEVEN fear to have the world, as they know it and are comfortable with it, disrupted. They fear violence, aggression or any movement toward them that might have the power to knock them off balance. It is interesting to note that even in something as innocent as a snowball fight they are extremely and noticeably guarded and fearful.

They fear the unknown, the unexpected. There is great need for them to see where they are going. On a trust walk they would peek! Being asked to fall back into another's arms would be so difficult for them that they would need to look to be sure the other is there ready to receive them.

There can exist in these types fear of letting go of planned movements. The head centered persons might find it hard to move into the flow of typing, and let go of the thinking about each letter in the task; hard to surrender to the leader in a dance; hard to come to the place of skill in speaking a foreign language that means ceasing to translate word by word.

How do these persons move best into the quiet and depths needed to be their real selves before God or to be present to the presence of God, as we earlier defined genuine prayer? What is their way of centering? Of coming to harmony and peace within themselves?

The head centered persons, living in their own inner space much of the time, experience within themselves an elaborate inner city. There is much richness within, ideas to be explored, plans to be developed, possibilities to be entertained, palaces to be visited. Entering into prayer for them, being present to the presence of God, is a question of restraining the natural desire that comes in the quiet to listen to and to follow the many voices within that begin to clamor for attention.

A way of genuine focused meditation[1] is the only route for the head centered person. It would require the keeping open of one's eyes, using the natural preference of the visual for life's connections and focusing on an outer object such as a cross, candle or Eucharist. The dispersed self that could so easily be

given to inner wandering is collected in the act of gazing. The inner and outer world of the person
somehow come together and the person experiences a
more unified stance. There is, in the gazing, a kind of
attempt to become one with the external object by
seeking to interiorize it or to project one's experience
onto it. Personal subjectivity then, tends to fall into
quiet and peace.

This approach to centering restrains the spontaneity of the person praying, which would lead them
to follow any of the thousands of ideas or insights
clamoring for attention within, and holds the person
in a focused state as the person gazes at the symbol.
This is a way of finding one's personal center.

The particular symbol or mandala chosen has its
own significance. Many of our symbols have been
created from a depth of human experience and contemplation. The symbol itself can evoke its source
and lead the person to his or her deepest self.

Some head centered persons choose to create
their own mandalas, usually a circular drawing containing various symbolic representations of the life
and world of the drawer. When one prays with a per-
sonally created mandala, it is a process of dwelling
upon one's own deepest identity mirrored in the symbol that is entered into. This dwelling saves the persons from the inherent danger of continuing to
ruminate in the time of prayer and remaining totally
unfocused.

In many ways, the prayer with the symbol or
mandala is stark. It is coming to realities needed in all
prayer: namely, that to pray we must desire God intensely to the point of seeking nothing else. The

possibility of this kind of desire is gift and only gift. To seek God and only God, not thoughts about God or answers to life's questions, is demanding, and at the same time supremely generous and self-transcendent. We need to be graced for that kind of generosity and love.

The continuous temptation for the head centered pray-ers is to go with the multitudinous ideas and thoughts that clamor for attention and to remain uncentered. It is prayer of denial when the mandala is used. It seems to be saying "no" to so much that is good and worthy of pursuit in order to respond to the greater gift given, the call to give attention purely to God.

The symbol or the mandala becomes like a screen for the meditator to project onto some aspect of the desire for God. The quality of the screen has some value. A symbol should be chosen carefully and kept to. It would be important to keep it simple so that the beauty of it or its complexity would not militate against the simple gazing. If the mandala is too complicated, it can do exactly the opposite of what one hopes it will make possible. It can be the source of many thoughts and ideas and simple gazing at it can become almost impossible. It can be good to move into the centering with the symbol in a quiet room that is neither too bright nor too dark. The symbol, then, will be neither too sharply delineated nor too obscure to gaze on. Repeated contemplations with the same mandala or symbol give the symbols a quality of greater depth and greater possibilities of mediating the centeredness desired.[2]

The use of a mantra or the use of a repeated

word or phrase is also very centering for the head centered person. The familiar path of mantra use where the word is chosen and repeated in one's depths without reflection on the meaning of the word is not helpful. Most helpful would be the auditory use of the word or words chosen. Oral repetition of the word, title of God or phrase is helpful. Important also is the attention given to the words themselves. Focusing on the meaning of the words concentrates the inner world of the head centered person. The focusing can lead to a greater and greater detachment from the noise within with which the head centered person struggles. As the mantra is whispered, said or sung or just listened to on a tape, the heart should be thinking of its meaning. The mind will come to quiet and reside in the heart. Tapes such as the Taize chants can be very good for these persons.

The Jesus Prayer, ("Jesus, Son of David, have mercy on me!" Mk 10,47) recited with reverence and attention can be a source of genuine inner stillness and singlemindedness for the numbers FIVE, SIX, SEVEN. Still, a third centering method for the head center of the Enneagram would be repetitive body movement, movement that mediates a sense of the inner depths and feeling of the person praying. Spontaneous, expressive dance will focus the persons on the realities of the heart and give some freedom from the tyranny of their own ideas, thoughts, plans or fears. Often, just watching liturgical dance can be very centering for the head centered person and something they tend to naturally appreciate.

When centered and focused on God, the head

centered persons find themselves seeking a union with God through the desire to know and to do His/Her will. It is rare that a number FIVE, SIX, SEVEN will find themselves being able to see any need to get angry with God. Suggestions to do so made by spiritual directors are often hard for these persons to understand or relate to. They see God as the author of universal law and appreciate its value. The aberrations of human life are often lain at the door of humans, whose deviance or folly seems logically to the head centered person, to be the true cause of pain and evil. Physical diminishment is viewed as part of the inbuilt corruption of all life. Their experience relates closely to that spoken of in Romans 8: 18-25. The head centered person experiences the harmony and beauty of life when it is lived according to God's designs and seeks to come into harmony with the will of God, which for them is but another way of naming God.

Another striking feature of head centered prayer is that these persons will naturally move in their prayer from universal concepts to what is more particular. Taking a universal command such as to "love as I have loved" and to move from that universal demand into a particular situation of their lives in which that command is challenging is quite natural to this center.

In the use of scripture, the head centered person doesn't naturally fall into imaginative prayer or affective prayer. There often tends to be a natural focusing on a line or phrase of a passage. The words chosen are assimilated in the manner of the mantra. More and more attention, deeper and deeper reflection should be given to the meaning of the words that attract. The result will be that the persons find themselves becoming more deeply detached from their own egos or thoughts about God and life and more able to stand centered in God's truth.

As head centered persons enter the word and world of God through the reading of scripture, they seek to find in it their own life or experience. This again is the syntony instinct or the strong desire they have for connection and harmony.

A spiritual issue that often surfaces with head centered persons who give themselves over seriously to the spiritual life is the theme of Exodus. Lands of slavery are named and desires for liberation and freedom become strong. The faces of slavery could be very varied. They could range from unquestioned beliefs, insincere relationships and dishonest securities. These personality types will seek to move with honesty and clarity from their places of false worship and become more willing to pass through their own particular deserts on the way to freedom.

In their efforts to pray, to come to freedom, to find God's will, the head centered personalities are willing to trust a road map. They do not have to be pioneers and discover it all for themselves. So they will put themselves in the paths of the spiritual greats, e.g., St. Theresa of Avila, St. John of the Cross, St. Catherine of Siena, St. Ignatius of Loyola, etc., and sit at the feet of the masters. They also explore with abundant fruit the spiritual classics, e.g., *The Autobiography of St. Theresa of Avila, Interior Castle* (by the same author), *The Ascent of Mt. Carmel, The Dark Night* (St. John of The Cross), etc., eagerly desirous of drinking from the wells of wisdom contained within the writings.

Simple structures of prayer can often be experienced as useful and freeing for them. They would tend to appreciate the order of the Church's liturgical year and adapt fruitfully to it. The structure is a means of focus again for persons often unfocused within. They would not experience the need to reconstruct totally the divine office should they be preparing for a community setting. Established forms would offer them a way to focus and to reach more deeply into the wealth of meaning in the world of the scripture or, in particular, the psalter. In general, it is easy for the head centered numbers to use established forms and within them to find ways of coming to depths, meaning and a genuine in-touchness with God.

If a person in this center chose a spiritual director, he/she would tend to move with caution, but once having done so would trust the person they perceived as being capable of directing them. There would be an almost childlike quality of surrender to suggestions made by the director if these seemed at all logical.

CHAPTER FIVE
Heart Centered Prayer: Expressive Prayer

In describing the approach to life of the head centered personality, the image of a violinist was used. (See Chapter 4). In the interests of continuing the musical imagery, one might describe the heart centered person not as the violinist, but rather as the violin. Life pulls the strings of the heart centered persons and it is from the energy of the outer world that their responses come. Fingers of need, of value judgments and of social expectations play upon the lives of the TWOS, THREES and FOURS. The strings of each of these numbers are tuned with a particular sensitivity. The TWOS are sensitive to need; the THREES to others' judgments of their achievements and the FOURS to others' views of their feelings.

The senses that are most highly developed in these persons are the senses of taste and touch. They seem to have continually in their mouths the taste of the experience of others' views of them and others' expectations of them. They are never untouched by others. It would be extremely difficult for them just to move on without giving space and reflection to the ways that others experience them. Inherent in our imagery and descriptive of the heart centered approach to life is the control that the outer world has upon this center. The ego of this center is described as the image ego and with significant reason. They live with questions that are real questions of image: Who am I with? Who helps? Who likes people? Are you going to like me or not?

These personalities struggle to be with themselves. The unexplored areas of human life for them are the highways and secret places of their own inner selves.

Their goodness or badness is often judged by others' response to them. It is this way of judging that leads them to accept affection so readily and easily. They feel accepted and valued if others respond lovingly and warmly toward them and express that warmth in touching their lives either physically or psychologically. A sense of inner integrity and harmony can be blurred by the degree of importance the heart centered person can give to the other's aproval and love. Conversely, there is a strong rejection of aggression in these persons. Aggression is judged most frequently as saying: "You are not all right;" "You have not measured up to my standards of helpfulness, success or refinement." The judgment of the success of the idealizations in the heart center comes very much from the outer world rather than from within as in some of the other personality types.

This center is extremely relational. Adjectives such as socially conscious, person oriented, and subjective are apt descriptives for these persons. In Jungian terminology, the feminine characteristic might easily be applied to them rather than the masculine. All in all there is a deep concern for the opinions of others.

The control of the outer world on these personalities is evidenced in yet another area of life. In their style of dress the heart centered persons tend to be adapters. They will feel the need to conform to the latest styles and be mod in their choice of clothes. The statement, "you might as well be dead as out of style," would have some resonance in them. Of the three heart centered numbers the TWOS are perhaps the least affected in this area and this only because the need to be attentive to others' needs can be so strong that they do not give sufficient reflection to their own image in the area of dress.

Because these numbers are constantly poised to receive messages and signals from the outside world they live with a great deal of anxiety. There is in them a constant free-floating anxiety that they will not be sensitive to the directives of life; that they will not be equal to the expectations of the other. This anxiety or positioning of one's self to receive directives from the outer world can cripple spontaneity and creativity. Risking non-approval would be paramount to risking ultimate security in the heart center.

Anxiety can surface strongly when these persons

are alone or are anticipating being alone. Who will give me my directives? How will the music of my life be freed if there is no one to touch the strings of life for me? Who will hear my music and appreciate it in my solitude? The thought of something like a long retreat or desert experience can be frightening to one who has become used to an outer world peopled with persons who give one worth and critiquing and in that energy for action. Inner emptiness is feared: the inner journey sometimes terrifies, and paralysis can be a possible result of solitude for the heart centered person who has not come to know their own inner resources.

In order to risk the terror of the inner world, the heart centered person must come to know the truth of the words of the Whiteheads in *Seasons of Strength.*

> Self intimacy is a virtue by which I grow in awareness and acceptance of this particular human being I am becoming. It is a strength of mature self-love which is the ground for my love and care for the other.[1]

A great enemy of this journey within, which for the heart centered personality can be a journey to self intimacy, is the over engagement with the outer world and the entry into an extremely active life. Brother David Steindl-Rast writes in *Gratefulness, the Heart of Prayer,* of this danger that could well be reflected upon by the TWOS, THREES and FOURS:

> Our activities create something like a centrifugal force. They tend to pull us from our center into peripheral concerns. And the faster the spin of our daily round of activities, the stronger the pull. We need to counteract it by anchoring ourselves in the silent center of our heart.[2]

Heart centered persons know, in their deepest selves, the call to anchor themselves in their hearts. And yet, they struggle to find ways to do that, ways to resist the pull of the outer world.

God reveals Himself/Herself to them as dwelling in the depths of their hearts. For them prayer begins by listening to the "Still, small voice of God" dwelling within and calling them to leave the outer world and its demands and to rest in one's own truth. It is an invitation to pass through gates that lead to an often unexplored world within. The passage through the gates is too narrow to take along bundles of preconceptions of ways to travel. There is no predetermined course of action in the way to approach the inner world. What is required for prayer in the heart center is a willingness to go where one has not traveled before and to go without a road map. The travel will require a sensitivity to one's own unprogrammed spontaneity. This spontaneity will express itself in intuitions, feelings and desires. Prayer will begin when the heart centered persons become truly aware of the world within themselves. The awareness for them is not the awareness of an outer meditation object such as the mandala for the head centered person, but the awareness of their own inner world. Their meditation objects become their own angers, worries, joys and fears. When these appear they should be accepted and attended to with a deep awareness that can eventually lead to a comprehension of their source and meaning. Prayer does not mean just analyzing feelings. Prayer is prayer when God and the person praying are in the prayer together. Otherwise, it could degenerate into a simple experience of introspection. It is important for the heart centered person to have a posture of greater and greater preparedness to become aware of their own inner state, but at the same time a posture of greater and greater transparency to God and willingness to let God preside over all their inner states. It cannot be emphasized too strongly that heart centered persons must be willing to be guided by the promptings of their own deeper nature and attend to their own, not others' perceptions. They must claim the right to author their own inner lives.

There is no need as in the head center to dwell on a fixed object or a verbal repetition. It is rather a dwelling upon or a contemplation of spontaneously arising imagery. Spontaneity is a key word in this method of centering. It is a way of unfolding, a way of letting happen which could be compared with the natural process of breathing. We can become aware sometimes of what we do so naturally and unreflectively in our ordinary breathing. In becoming aware, we must try not to manipulate the breath.[3]

The basic rule in heart centered prayer is self-expression. The goal is that of letting the true self identity emerge, not the identity taken on to please others. It is in sustained effort to become aware in prayer of one's feelings and emotions that, for the sincerely spiritual person, will give rise to genuine freedom of self-expression and authentic Christian witness. It is then and only then that the real self can stand before God unprotected and transparent. So desirous was this kind of self-expression that sometimes in non-Christian religions it was achieved through the use of drugs.

> Drugs have been traditionally employed as catalysts to achieve self-expression and prophetic attitudes.[4]

In our Christian perspective we are not recommending the use of drugs but simply note the intended effect for persons who are blocked in their image consciousness by others' opinions. Drugs can release this form of slavery to the outer world but, all would agree, can also result in another form of dependence.

In the approach to scripture there is a great difference from the approach of the head centered person. The routes traveled to touch the truth of God's word are entirely different. For the head center it is the way of form. When entering the scriptures the following is the reality:

> The way of form is based upon the predication: Here is truth; assimilate it; make it your own.[5]

The words within the heart center tell them:

> The truth lies within you, and you can find it only by forgetting ready made answers.[6]

Both centers come to the truth of God's word by routes that are particularly suited to the energy and needs of their ways of being with self and the world.

Another significant difference in the ways of praying the scriptures is in the fact that the head centered person will begin with a universal truth and come to the particularization of it in one's own life. The heart centered person, on the contrary, will be encouraged to begin with a particular experience of life and then touch the universal principle. An example of this would be the importance of the TWO, THREE, FOUR being able to stay with the pain of a relationship. From the starting point of that particular experience and all that it evokes, they then come to the word of God in the scriptures that speaks to the inner feeling and emotions of the person praying. The heart centered person, with the encouragement to spontaneously go with the flow of life and feeling in prayer can also, with great fruit, read a scripture passage and just let their imaginations carry them. Ignatian meditation, or just slipping into a scene, can be natural for them and extremely meaningful.

Expressive prayer, or the prayer from one's own center, will lead the pray-er to a kind of self assurance and self possession that is extremely freeing. These persons will then be able to allow personal creativity to emerge and will be able to move beyond outer structures and established ways of doing things. The heart centered person knows the echo deep within that is a constant call to this kind of freedom. They know the need to become more and more aware of their conditioning by the outer world and the corresponding call to think their own thoughts, to feel their own feelings and ultimately to make their own decisions.

Dreams can be for the heart centered persons an excellent means for touching the deeper world within. In sleep one often has access to the repressed emotions and concerns of one's waking moments. By paying attention to dreams and by reflecting on the gifts they hold out, one can be led to gratefully take hold of their wisdom and truth. In so doing, one is taking hold of one's inner world. There are many excellent and readable works on dreams available to the reader such as *Dreams and Spiritual Growth*[7] by Louis Savary and others or *Dreams and Healing*[8] by John Sanford. It would be particularly worthwhile for the heart centered persons of the Enneagram to study the discipline of dream analysis. They of all the personality types of the Enneagram need the most help in coming to touch their own inner world. Some basic tools are often sufficient to make it possible to profit from the wisdom of one's dreams. One such simple technique is to approach the dream as a whole. Give your dream a *Title.* Let it come spontaneously as an answer to the question, "What would I entitle this dream?" Secondly, name the *Theme* of the dream, recall all the major themes or issues which surfaced within it. If there is more than one, note them in order. Thirdly, identify the *Affect*, report all the dominant feelings or emotional energies experienced in the dream. If they follow a sequence, note that as well. Finally, the dream confronts you with a *Question.* What question is it asking of you? What is your dream trying to help you be conscious of? This technique is popularly called TTAQ by Savary and Berne in *Dreams and Spiritual Growth* pp. 22-24.

The question of distractions is one that is often dwelt upon when one speaks of or writes about prayer. The recommended handling of distractions in the head and heart centers of the Enneagram is very different. The way of discipline was recommended for the head centered persons. They have a spontaneous urge to pursue the ideas and images that present themselves in prayer, thus risking the loss of focus and centeredness they seek.

Remembering that the way of unrestraint and spontaneity is key to heart centered prayer, it will be important for them to follow their distractions. Being image conscious, they will receive from the outer world voices that will tell them that distractions are not good. These will come not from their own depths but from outside, and there will be a tendency to resist distractions. It is in following them that these persons can come in touch with what is authentic within. Important to note, however, is the fact that all distractions are not of equal importance. Some are like flies, bothersome more than anything else. They are the small details of life that flit through everyone's prayer. These should be let go. To spend one's time swatting flies is useless. More important distractions are the ones that heart centered persons are encouraged to welcome and explore. These would be thoughts about one's relationships, one's future, one's feelings, etc. To travel down the road of one's distractions can lead to one's center, to one's truth.

Prayer that allows for ecstacy and enthusiastic self-expression is an excellent form for heart-centered persons. Charismatic prayer has been notably popular with such persons. It has the features of community and spontaneity which are so characteristic of the needs in the heart center. Charismatic prayer would be natural for them while at the same time much less popular among the head centered persons. To let one's life unfold, to reverence one's own process is very important for the TWO, THREE and

FOUR. It is to know that in the unfolding one comes to God and to fullness of life rather than in "putting on" values and roles that society can impose.

It can be hard for this center to act, even in prayer, in accordance with their preferences. They can continually act out of community or church expectations, never knowing why prayer is always experienced as straining and always feeling inauthentic before God. In a directed retreat, the heart centered persons can be overly conscious of the expectations of the director and unconsciously work toward attaining the prayer experience that they imagine will please the director rather than attend to the authentic leadings of the Spirit of God. God's Spirit will often lead them deeply into their own lives and the unexpected results will not always seem to fit with what they have interpreted as the expected outcomes of their prayer. It is extremely important in spiritual direction or retreat direction for the TWO, THREE or FOUR *to risk being themselves.* This kind of non-judgmental forum will provide for them an initial experience of being accepted as they really are. It is an experience that can be strengthening in the process of risking transparency in other forums of life.

It is not only in the area of human relationships that the heart centered personalities struggle to be authentic. We have all heard the statement: "You relate to God as you relate to others." The image ego of the center leads persons to come before God in the ways they have idealized themselves. The TWO is constantly trying to see how indeed God can be assisted in the work of responding to the needs of the world. The THREE tries to maintain the image of success in ministry and relationships and would find it so difficult, even in this most intimate forum, to pray the pain of failure or betrayal. The heightened expression of feeling can lead the FOUR in prayer to attend to the psuedo feelings with which life is approached rather than being simple and in-touch before God.

The creative world of the Spirit of God within the human heart has to be reverenced and carefully attended to. In the heart center, the Spirit of God competes with so many other voices the person has become used to listening to.

Heart centered persons need to be encouraged to face and explore their doubts. This can be very frightening for them because of the fear they feel that such exploration will lead them to express themselves in unacceptable ways. This coming face to face with doubt and truth is the only path to authentic life for this center. One's demons need also to be faced and named. It is only in the naming that control is gained. Thomas Merton is said to have suggested to his novices imagery that could be very helpful in this area. He asked them to imagine they were standing before a deep, dark pool. The pool had monsters lurking in its depths. They were to gaze at the waters of the pool until one by one each monster had come up for air. After a period of time, they would have seen and named each monster. In the naming, they would be able to control what was in the sinister depths and not be surprised by what might emerge. This pool was the inner world of the novice. Heart centered persons are often taken by surprise by their own angers, prides, or jealousies. Because they have not walked regularly the terrain within, they do not know what lurks in the depth. Coming to know the demons is the first step in learning to speak with them and eventually being able to allow the energy they embody to become a creative energy.

Discernment of spirits is also vital in the heart center. Discernment is simply a process of sifting out. Much has been written on this topic, so we will be brief. It is based on the recognition of the scriptural reality in I John 4, 1-3 that it is not every spirit that we can trust. There is a need to test them. The TWOS, THREES and FOURS need to sift out the spirits moving within them. They need to reflect on the fingers that are plucking the strings of their lives and make decisions about what is indeed graced and what is demonic. This is not possible without a sincere entry into the expressive prayer described in this chapter.

CHAPTER SIX
Gut Centered Prayer
(Quiet Prayer)

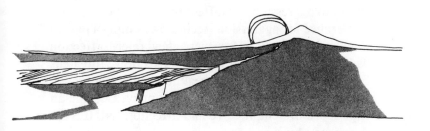

An extremely simple kind of prayer is suitable to gut centered people (EIGHT, NINE, ONE). It is the way of quiet. The energy of these people is intense and immediate. They react quickly to things and situations out of the motivation to control reality by power (EIGHTS), by remaining settled and free from conflict (NINES) or by being right, making something right (ONES). People in this center are a high energy group. The powerfulness, passionate striving for justice (their own and others' rights), love, truth and excitement of the EIGHTS and the relentless striving and trying harder for a world of truth, justice and moral perfection of the ONES easily portrays this energy. NINES appear calm and unflappable, seemingly in a stupor or drugged. However, this state is won at a great cost, for it takes a great deal of energy to drain conflict from both their inner life and their life situation in the outer world. Thus, energy becomes an issue for these people and they can appear drained of energy and unwilling to move from their planted position. As we will see later in the chapter each in its own way needs to let reality be, to let go. Another characteristic of this center which makes this prayer helpful is their attitude to aggression and affection. These people have a tolerance for aggression, seeing it as simply a part of the world as it is. However, they reject affection which does threaten them. Affection threatens EIGHTS as they avoid weakness and tenderness, which are for them a real loss of control. Lacking an experience of genuine love and affection, NINES are threatened by it and can resist it as unimportant, not such a big deal. ONES resist affection because they are never perfect enough to have merited it.

Anger is the emotion least controlled in this center. Anger in the EIGHTS appears to be easily expressed and then they move on with life. In the NINES anger is often controlled, pushed down, but when the practice of turning off strong feelings no longer works, their anger can be forceful, even volatile. Surprisingly, NINES can be the angriest of them all. ONES have a lot of anger at the imperfect world. But as it is not right for a good boy or girl to express it, anger builds up in them in the form of resentment. It comes out in passive-aggressive ways or in reaction formation.

Prayer

The way of quiet is an excellent prayer for these people. It is good for them simply to come in faith into the presence of God and just sit. The stance in prayer is one of a simple, quiet, peaceful abiding in God's Presence. In this practice, they enter more deeply into the mystery of Christ's death and resurrection. St. John Vianney once asked an old man who spent hours daily in church what he did during all that time. "I don't do anything," he replied. "I just look at Him and He looks at me." An echo of that beautiful expression was spoken by the old man in Ireland of whom Edward Farrell wrote. He had asked: "What are you doing?" And the old man answered: "I am just sitting here because the Father is very fond of me."

Those statements capture the heart of this prayer. The old man was not saying, doing or thinking anything. He simply sat there and let God look at him with love. This kind of prayer was one Teresa of Avila used to recommend to her sisters.[1] In a relationship of love the partners like to gaze lovingly on the face of the beloved. This prayer avoids ideas, concepts or images. It neither prays in reflective meditation nor expresses one's own inner energy and feelings before God. Quiet prayer helps gut centered people bring together their inner and outer worlds through minimizing the use of words, thoughts and images, or eliminates words, images and thoughts altogether. This is the kind of prayer that St. John of the Cross speaks of in his *Dark Night of the Senses* or the author of *The Cloud of Unknowing* explains in that remarkable work.

> This is what you are to do: lift your heart up to the Lord,
> with a gentle stirring of love desiring him for his own sake
> and not for his gifts. Center all your attention and desire on
> him and let this be the sole concern of your mind and heart.
> Do all in your power to forget everything else, keeping your
> thoughts and desires free from involvement with any of
> God's creatures or their affairs whether in general or in par-
> ticular.[2]

This way of centering on God involves another form
of communication. In expressive prayer or meditation
the pray-er employs thoughts, feelings, plans or images, etc., and at the same time continues to learn
about God through pondering the Scriptures. These
vehicles of communication can sometimes impede
rather than foster our communion or intimacy with
God. Silence—of words, thoughts and images—can
be a powerful form of communication with God
when hearts are mutually moved by love.

Restless Mind

This communication with God from our center,
our core, is no simple matter. Unfortunately, human
persons cannot turn off their thinking and imagination by some gesture of flicking a switch. In fact, our
minds keep thoughts and images streaming before us.

> . . . no sooner has a man turned toward God in love when
> through human frailty he finds himself distracted by the
> remembrance of some created thing or some daily care. But
> no matter. No harm is done; for such a person quickly
> returns to deep recollection.[3]

These thoughts, words and images attract us and grab
our attention, drawing us away from centering and

quiet prayer. In some way or other they have a hold on us. Our hearts are attached to them, hold them dear (power for the EIGHTS; being settled for the NINES; being right for the ONES), or fear them (weakness and tenderness for the EIGHTS; conflict and inner turmoil for the NINES; and resentment for the ONES), or in some way are a reality with which we are intensely involved.

To silence the mind with its constant thinking is a very difficult task. A way that can prove beneficial is to use one thought to chase the other thoughts, or an image which will remove the other thoughts and images which crowd in for our attention. Fasten on one thought or phrase, or sentence, or word or image. Trying to keep the mind empty is a fruitless exercise. Since it must occupy itself with something, give it just *one* thing: a word or ejaculation which you repeat to keep the mind from wandering, or an image of the Lord Jesus on which you look lovingly and to which you return when distracted. A time will come when you will leave the image or thoughts behind and go to God abiding in your depths.

> If you want to gather all your desire into one simple word that the mind can easily retain, choose a short word rather than a long one. A one-syllable word such as "God" or "love" is best. But choose one that is meaningful to you. Then fix it in your mind so that it will remain there come what may. This word will be your defense in conflict and in peace. Use it to beat upon the cloud of darkness above you and to subdue all distractions, consigning them to the *cloud of forgetting* beneath you. Should some thought go on annoying you demanding to know what you are doing, answer with this one word alone. If your mind begins to intellectualize over the meaning and connotations of this little word, remind yourself that its value lies in its simplicity. Do

> this and I assure you these thoughts will vanish. Why?
> Because you have refused to develop them with arguing.[4]

God will be known in that silent gazing in darkness, not in light. People who silence the thoughts will complain that they are doing nothing, wasting their time at prayer. It is a time of faith, of pure bare attention to God. It is also a time of dying to our thoughts, images and feelings and focusing our attention on God. Anthony de Mello gives a description of this prayer and some of its effects on those who persevere in it.

> If they avoid this evil (abandoning prayer) and persevere in
> the exercise of prayer and expose themselves, in blind faith,
> to the emptiness, the darkness, the idleness, the
> nothingness, they will gradually discover, at first in small
> flashes, later in a more permanent fashion, that there is a
> glow in the darkness, that the emptiness mysteriously fills
> their heart, that the idleness is full of God's activity, that in
> the nothingness their being is recreated and shaped anew
> . . . and all of this in a way they just cannot describe either
> to themselves or to others. They will just know after each
> session of prayer or contemplation, call it what you will,
> that something mysterious has been working within them,
> bringing refreshment and nourishment and well-being with
> it. They will notice they have a yearning hunger to return to
> this dark contemplation that seems to make no sense and
> yet fills them with life . . .[5]

Detachment

Gut centered prayer, like that of head and heart, moves to union with God through a dying and rising. It is an entering into the experience of the Passion, Death and Resurrection of Jesus. It is not our true self, our deepest self as imaging our God, which dies, but rather the illusion that our ego is all powerful and can be its own security. As we surrender this illusion, we grow in greater dependence on God. An ascesis of detachment best fosters this union with God, prepares the ground for the influx of God's gifts. The EIGHT needs to become free from the attachment to the abuse of power manifested in bullying others, controlling and dominating situations, and power plays. EIGHTS also need moderation of their passionate pursuit for justice when this leads them to oversensitivity to real or imagined injuries to their own rights and those of others. In such situations they can be aggressive and punishing of others. EIGHTS can be attached to the feeling of and expression of anger, like to a stimulating shower. They can use it and overstimulation with fast cars, sports, dangerous activities, as ways of alleviating boredom. EIGHTS need detachment from such excess. NINES need detachment from the search to stay calm and settled, their "peace at any price" posture. NINES try to overcome feelings of boredom and purposelessness by all sorts of external stimulating activities. They can appear as busy people, going from one trivial activity to another. Their restless searching moves NINES to seek in workshops, counselors, spiritual guides or gurus the answers to their lives. They need a freedom which enables them to overcome their laziness about engaging in the interior journey. Their attachment to keeping conflict down or from getting within them leads them to procrastination, failure to set priorities or accept responsibility for their choices. ONES need detachment from their relentless, driven quest for an 'unreal or

and is now ready to receive the seed that is sown. This attitude of openness disposes them to welcome whatever the Lord may bring or give.

From what has been said, one can see that detachment in prayer and detachment in everyday life go hand in hand. This is strikingly pointed out in an incident in the life of Zen Master Bokusan:

> During the civil disturbances of the nineteenth century a fugitive samurai took refuge in the temple of Soto Zen Master Bokusan. Three pursuers arrived and demanded to know where he was. "No one here," said the Zen master. "If you won't tell us, then let's cut off your head," and they drew their swords to do so. "Then if I am to die," said the Zen master, "I think I'll have a little wine." And he took down a small bottle, poured it, and sipped with evident relish.
>
> The samurai looked at one another. Finally they went away. Bokusan was repeatedly asked about this incident, but did not want to discuss it. Once however he said: "Well, there is something to be learnt from it. When those fellows came, I did not do what they wanted, but neither did I quarrel with them or plead with them. I just gave up their whole world and had nothing to do with them. And after a time I found they had gone away.
>
> "Similarly when people complain that they are overwhelmed with passions and wrong thoughts, they should know that the right way is not to quarrel nor to plead or argue. Simply give up all claim on their world and have nothing to do with them, and after a time you will find that they have gone away."[6]

Christians know that that intimate "Abba Experience" is the source of Jesus' life and preaching. We find this story throwing light on a gesture in Jesus' life which has puzzled commentators. Once an attempt was made to trap Jesus by seeking his decision on the case of a woman caught in adultery (Jn 8, 1-11). At two junctures, Jesus bent down to write on the ground. What he wrote is not important. Is his gesture not an expression of detachment, a nonviolent love and serenity which unmasks and overpowers the righteous anger and lust within the accusers? We find it tempting to read it that way.

Preparation for Prayer

Since gut centered people are high energy persons, they will have to pay particular attention to slowing down, anticipating and desiring their time of prayer. The relationship of the little prince and the fox in the well known fairy tale, *The Little Prince,* has a lot to say to us in this regard. When the prince was on a strange planet, he met a fox. The little prince says that he is unhappy and would like the fox to play with him. "I cannot play with you," the fox said. "I am not tamed."[7] The prince does not understand what taming means and asks the fox to explain. The fox says:

> It is an act too often neglected, . . . It means to establish ties . . . To me, you are still nothing more than a little boy who is just like a hundred thousand other little boys. And I have no need of you. And you, on your part, have no need of me. To you I am nothing more than a fox like a hundred thousand other foxes. But if you tame me, then we shall need each other. To me, you will be unique in all the world. To you, I shall be unique in all the world . . .[8]

The fox relates further that he will then be able to know the prince's step which will be like music and the previously meaningless wheat field will remind him of his golden hair.

The fox then directly asks the prince to tame him if he wants a friend. And then he instructs him on the process of relationship:

> You must be very patient, . . . First you will sit down at a little distance from me—like that—in the grass. I shall look at you out of the corner of my eye, and you will say nothing. Words are the source of misunderstandings. But you will sit a little closer to me, every day . . .[9]

The prince receives further instruction in other rites of relationship which are like rules in prayer. Besides using one's life situation as a source for reminders of God, as the wheat field points to the blond headed prince, prayer is helped by regularity of time. The fox says:

> If, for example, you come at four o'clock in the afternoon, then at three o'clock I shall begin to be happy. I shall feel happier and happier as the hour advances. At four o'clock, I shall already be worrying and jumping about. I shall show you how happy I am! But if you come at just any time, I shall never know at what hour my heart is to be ready to greet you . . . One must observe the proper rites . . .[10]

Prayer requires some preparation, a disposing of oneself. Anticipation of prayer time can help slow a person down. If it is your custom to pray early in the morning, think of the time the night before. Let thoughts of God sink deeply within you as you rest at night, like the long process of soaking a rum raisin cake. As we are in a world in which our senses are constantly being bombarded by sights, sounds, etc., we need to focus our awareness to move into our depths.

Prayer and Sleep

Falling asleep is a condition which demands reflection relative to this quiet prayer, or any prayer for that matter. When the mind moves into an altered state of consciousness in prayer, the brainwaves slow down, moving from Beta consciousness in which the mind is actively attending and focused towards the outside world, to Alpha consciousness, where the internal state is one of relaxed awareness with a move towards interiority. Drowsiness (Theta Brainwaves) and sleep (Delta Brainwaves) are not far away from this very restful state. It can often be a struggle. especially for NINES, to remain awake and alert.

This deserves some reflection. As a general rule, in a person who is attempting to place himself/herself before the presence of God, falling asleep is not something to worry about. If our attitude is one of receiving all things from God, then we can thank God even for sleep. Our God loves us fully whether awake or asleep. On reawakening one can simply return gently to attentiveness to God's presence. If sleep is a regular occurrence, then it merits a further look. We can question if we are getting enough sleep. A common struggle for the dedicated minister or involved person is the attempt to do more than we should, crowding the days and weeks with too many engagements and tasks. Or perhaps we simply get too physically comfortable in this form of prayer. Consideration can be given then to observing our posture or moving to a more upright and less comfortable chair. If these possibilities do not fit our condition, then one can explore another avenue. Sleep may signal some resistance, e.g., to some area of our life which we are not facing such as poor self-image, inter-personal conflicts, etc., and keep us as well from deal-ing with a growing intimacy or closeness to God. If the latter is the case, then we will need to work on our relationship of trust in our loving God.

In sum, gut centered prayer is very different from heart centered and head centered prayer. It is a state of recognition that I have feelings, thoughts, am a bodily person, but I am not any of these. I am more than these. This prayer cultivates an awareness that one is attending to the presence of God. This way of prayer is preferred by gut centered persons. From time to time they will use meditation and ex-pressive prayer to communicate their feelings about something. It is not an exclusive way of prayer for them. The head and heart centered prayer forms will also lead them into a prayer of quiet. This is the normal movement of prayer, its way of development and deepening. These three ways of centering are the various centers' preferred ways of being before the presence of God and will follow the usual states of growth in prayer. The fox has another word of wisdom which portrays concretely the gut centered prayer. He says:

> It is the time you have wasted for your rose that makes your rose so important.[11]

It is the time that one wastes with one's God that is so important. Gut centered prayer can look like a waste of time. The test of it, as of all prayer, is whether we are growing more loving, compassionate, and humble, whether we are exemplifying in our lives the fruits of the Spirit (Ga 5, 22-23).

SUMMARY OF PRAYER OF THE CENTERS

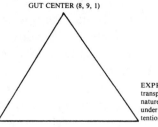

QUIET PRAYER: Silencing the mind, removal of thoughts, feelings, state of bare attention, emptiness, detachment, receptivity.

GUT CENTER (8, 9, 1)

HEART CENTER (2, 3, 4)

EXPRESSIVE PRAYER: Freedom, transparency, surrender to one's true nature. Allow the flow of energy buried under roles, programming, conscious intentions, inner directed.

HEAD CENTER (5, 6, 7)

FOCUSED MEDITATION: absorption, union, outer-directed. Discipline thoughts and feelings, focus attention on a fixed object or image.

WAYS
of
PRAYER
✝ FOR
LIFE's
JOURNEY

Dealing With One's Particular Avoidance

Each of the nine personality types has a particular area of avoidance. It is that dimension most opposed to and therefore most threatening to the idealization, our self image or self concept. Whatever does not fit the self's portrayal, its public mask, becomes a threat to the very definition of self. T.S. Eliot put it well: "We prepare a face to meet the faces that we meet." So with each personality certain experiences and situations which occasion them come to be feared. They are viewed as a threat to the survival of the ego. In other words, the personality believes itself to be the idealization ("I am powerful"—EIGHT; "I am settled"—NINE), so anything which would uncover or unmask that belief is perceived as life threatening.

The path to wholeness is to deal with one's avoidance. The adjective 'whole' according to Webster's Dictionary comes from the Old High German *heil*, meaning healthy and unhurt. These dimensions are included as we use it here in the sense of the fullness of nature or development. Each person is on the road towards that wholeness. Wholeness is achieved as one gradually befriends what is sensed as life threatening. It is a life long journey. This is a process and will take time, for we do not make friends with what is perceived as threatening overnight. We will need patience in this inner work. The Irish have a saying that runs something like this: "If you run from the ghost, it will chase you. If you turn and face it, it will run away." There is need on the way to wholeness to enter the desert land, the dark and unknown territory, of the avoidance. Working with the particular blind spot is a way out of the compulsive clinging to the idealization. It opens us to more of reality as we adopt a more open and less defensive posture to life. It also enables the personality types to develop their own giftedness, thus becoming more self-transcendent and loving.

The human psyche in order to preserve itself uses various defense mechanisms to exclude from awareness the threatening experience. Jung[1] used the term *shadow* to speak about the dark and unknown part of the psyche. It is that part of the person that contains all the unwanted and undeveloped aspects of the personality. The *shadow* is like another person in me. It has a personality all its own. I am unaware of these parts either because they are incompatible with my conscious ego or because they are potentials unknown to me. For Jung, dealing with the *shadow* is the work of the second half of life. In the first half of life he sees the human person primarily occupied with the development of a personal identity, as well as finding a particular place in life. Until the middle years we use most of our psychic energy to pursue these aims and whatever particular vocation we choose. Once we have achieved identity and have made an adequate adaptation to our vocation or life style, we begin to feel a new need for establishing integration or wholeness.

From our perspective we would not postpone the opportunity for movement to wholeness until the second half of life. Individuals who courageously face their avoidance, who befriend it, are on the path to wholeness. Entering that area is like being in a no man's land between the real self and the idealization. So working with one's blind spot is a way out of the compulsion. By engaging in this struggle a person develops his/her own particular giftedness and can be a source of encouragement and enlightenment for others. A conscious confronting of the avoidance is needed. We need to become familiar with it so that we can describe what it is like, what it wants and what it needs.

At this point, we will describe briefly the avoidance of each of the personality types and invite you to become familiar with the one with which you grapple.

Eight: Ego Vengeance
Idealization: "I am powerful;" "I can do."
Avoidance: Weakness and Tenderness

Deep within the EIGHT are feelings of weakness and tenderness. These, however, are feared because acknowledging them or letting others see them would leave them too vulnerable. So these persons try to maintain the outward appearance of toughness and hardness. When they are with persons or things who pose no threat to them, e.g., weak people, children, nature, or animals, they can let this dimension of weakness and tenderness become manifest. The giftedness of the EIGHT appears when their strength is flavored with tenderness and their weakness is integrated into their personality.

Nine: Ego Indolence
Idealization: "I am set;" "I am settled."
Avoidance: Conflict and Turmoil

NINES try to keep conflict out of inner and outer situations of life. Conflict would disturb their attempts to remain calm, so they expend great amounts of energy keeping conflict out of their lives. This leads to an affective life which is dormant as if their emotions were asleep in a rocking chair. The giftedness of the NINES emerges when their calm and tranquil appearance is integrated with some genuine passion for life and action, enabled by doing the work of the inner journey, facing the turmoil within them.

One: Ego Resentment
Idealization: "I am right;" "I am good."
Avoidance: Anger/Resentment

ONES have a lot of anger at the imperfection in themselves and in the world. Yet their countless "shoulds" tell them it is not right to be angry. So anger festers in them and can come out as resentment at the stupidity and imperfection around them. The giftedness of the ONES is heightened by facing their anger and having it transformed into energy for pursuit of truth, justice and moral perfection accompanied by an inner serenity.

Two: Ego Flattery
Idealization: "I am helpful;" "I can give."
Avoidance: Needs

The TWO personality finds identity in being a giver. Without it, these persons would cease to exist. Acknowledging their own needs is a struggle for them. They find it difficult to pay caring attention to their own life experience. The inner inadequacy which they feel compels them to multiply acts of service of others, to live in the outer and not the inner world. In the outer world, they desire others to receive their often compulsive giving, to like them or show appreciation in return. Yet others' responses never satisfy them. The giftedness of the TWOS in caring becomes more unselfish as they face their own needs and deal with them. They can then be truly sensitive to the real needs of others.

Three: Ego Vanity/Go-Go
Idealization: "I am successful;" "I am efficient."
Avoidance: Failure

The THREE personality finds worth in success. The job, role, career and image are what give them self definition. They fear failure in work, projects, and relationships because it seems to show them to be inadequate and incapable. Failure is generally viewed as a personal failure. The genuine giftedness of the THREE in accomplishing tasks, goals, leading or facilitating groups or individuals emerges as they face and deal with failure and their inner world. They can then offer others a sensitivity to their persons because they have become at-home with themselves.

Four: Ego Melancholy
Idealization: "I am special;" "I am sensitive, refined."
Avoidance: Simple joy or sadness

The FOUR, like other personalities of the heart center, tend to see themselves as on stage all the time. This means that they stand not only in the spotlight of others' eyes, but also in the light of their own self appraisal. They aim not so much at performance for others' sake but to present themselves satisfactorily as special, living by elite standards, or refined. This compulsion leads them to avoid simple joys or sadness. Ordinary reality—most of life—is feared by them because it may reveal life as incomplete, unfinished, ugly, tedious or humdrum. In facing everydayness and ordinary joys and sorrows the giftedness of the FOURS is enhanced in their appreciation of the world around them and their capacity to foster goodness and beauty in people and their surroundings.

Five: Ego Stinginess
Idealization: "I am wise;" "I am perceptive."
Avoidance: Emptiness

FIVES, like others in the head center, want to be connected with reality, people and events. They have a desire to know, to perceive reality so that they can know where they are with reality and other persons. They observe, watch and fill themselves up; but seldom do they engage in life or give forth their perceptions and observations. FIVES try to fill themselves up to avoid a haunting sense of inner emptiness. They feel small, of little importance, or lacking any original idea. In facing this inner emptiness, the giftedness of the FIVE in their open minded, curious, creative thinking can be shared with others.

Six: Ego Cowardice
Idealization: "I am faithful;" "I am loyal;" "I am obedient."
Avoidance: Deviance or Disobedience

The SIX personality tries to be faithful, loyal and obedient in thought and action. Fear and doubt plague their decisions and actions. They try to quiet this by strong dogmatic faith, following a leader, or having an external norm or reason to justify their line of thinking and conduct. To come to wholeness of personality and a full development of their giftedness, the SIX needs to walk into the darkness of deviance and disobedience. Their capacity to be warm-hearted friends and innovative leaders will then flourish. They need to become more inner directed and operate out of their own authority.

Seven: Ego Planner
Idealization: "I am OK;" "I am fine."
Avoidance: Pain

SEVENS try to maintain a happy, friendly and optimistic view about everything. To maintain this they plan and tend to avoid things that are painful, disruptive, negative or unpleasant. They seem to find pain of all forms, physical or psychological, as intolerable. For their giftedness of possessing creative vision, being celebrators of life and communicators of goodness—present—everywhere, to develop, they need to face the darkness and negative experiences of life.

EXERCISES
A. Dialogue With The Area Of Avoidance

The goal of facing the avoidance is not to eliminate it but rather to integrate it. Wholeness is never achieved by cutting away a part of ourselves. One cannot simply get rid of the dark side, the unacceptable dimension. This avoidance area needs to be worked with; otherwise the particular personality will lack depth and richness. Achieving some integration enables us to fill out our personalities and makes us more fully human and alive. Confronting, dialoguing with the avoidance has the effect of freeing us from its negative and compulsive power.

Dialogue is a relationship in which there is a mutual meeting of persons, each one accepting, speaking and most importantly listening to one another. There is also the possibility of an inner dialogue[2] within a person's life. This involves the inner relationship between the different aspects of an individual's life.

In dialogue it is good to relax and be still. Then you use your imagination and choose to whom or what you want to speak. You write down what comes without editing, writing for an audience, staging it or controlling it. You need to let it happen rather than force it. You can dialogue with virtually anything or everything. To dialogue with your area of avoidance you can imagine this aspect of yourself as present, perhaps personify it, even give it a name. Then allow the dialogue to take place in the mind and set it down on paper. The two parties are allowed to speak to one another. As in dialogue with persons it takes time to be comfortable with one another. You may experience this in your initial attempts. Here is a dialogue that a ONE might do in facing anger.

JOHN—I dread doing this. I am afraid of looking at you, ANGER. I don't quite know what to do or expect in this and wonder if I will get it right. In fact, I feel a bit foolish. One thing is clear to me though: I have been for a long time uneasy with you, ANGER.

ANGER—It is good, finally, to be talking with you, JOHN. I have been part of your life but have always felt like a wicked step-sister—someone shunned and hidden away. You never were comfortable with me. Yet I mean you no harm.

JOHN—That last statement seems rich to me. I know that I have never liked you. You got me into more trouble—with my parents, in school and out on the playground. I never quite knew what to do with you . . .

Another example is this dialogue of a SEVEN with pain.

PAIN—BARBARA, I keep touching your life. You keep ignoring my presence.

BARBARA—I don't like you. You intrude upon my ability to keep things moving, productive and happy.

PAIN—I am an important part of your life. I give you indications of troubles in your body, stress in your mind or spirit. I could become your friend, your very good friend if you would stop running from me.

BARBARA—I often don't believe what you tell me. Sometimes I notice you and you go away and I'm glad I didn't stop over you.

PAIN—What you say is true, but most often it is very important to listen to me.

BARBARA—I'll try to hear you a bit more.

PAIN—There are other ways I come. I accompany your losses, disappointments, and griefs. I touch you deeply at such times. I let you know how important it is for you to care for yourself, to take time.

BARBARA—I hate just to feel sorry for myself. I find that if "I get going," things get better.

PAIN—In running from me you run the risk of being very superficial. If you listen to my warnings, sit with me, a depth will come, a deeper appreciation of what others live with. I can bring you a deep spirit of compassion which will enrich your bright, happy personality.

BARBARA—I will try to trust you more and stay with you instead of running. I know its going to take

a while to get to be comfortable with you because I think it's so important not to let you show. I'm going to find it hard to let others see that we are becoming friends. . . .
Let the dialogue go on until it naturally comes to some ending.

There are three further suggestions that may deepen the experience of the dialogue and enable you to derive more benefit:
1) If the dialogue is written in such a way that it has an I-you form, you can reverse the pronouns when rereading it aloud. Reading it aloud enables you very often to sense more of the depth of the dialogue and catch its feeling tone. Sometimes a burst of insight comes forth in this new reading.
2) In rereading the dialogue aloud, notice whether any of the voices sound familiar. Listening in this way you may be able to identify some of the voices of your past or present (parents, significant others, teachers, society, Church) which you have internalized and made your own. Such recognition, awareness about the sources of judgments of our thinking and feeling, can give us more power of choice to listen to them or not and freedom to listen to our own truth.
3) Finally, this dialogue can be very powerful when done in the presence of Jesus. You can place yourself in his presence and then do the dialogue. You can read it to him. You can allow him to interact with the parties of the dialogue and be a participant as you dialogue with the area of avoidance. We read of him in John's Gospel:

"All that came to be had life in Him and that life was the
light of men, a light that shines in the dark, a light that
darkness could not overpower." Jn 1, 4-5

Befriending our avoidance in this way can be a
significant help on the path to wholeness. We will
gradually discover that it is not as threatening to our
true self as we once thought and we will find ourselves
able to embrace more of ourselves in the process and
begin to reach out more in compassion to others. In
time we will experience that we need not defend
ourselves so strongly in this area. And slowly what
will dawn is the truth that facing the awareness is not
only a path to wholeness; it is also a privileged place
where we meet our God.

B. Imaging The Avoidance

Some of the personality types of the Enneagram
will find themselves more at home and have an easier
capacity for inward perception (i.e., head centered
persons) than others (particularly difficult for heart
centered persons). Moreover, our lives tend to be so
busy and we receive so much pressure from the outer
environment that moving into our depth in stillness
may be little used. Yet it is a native human capacity.
Imaging[3] the avoidance can have an enlightening,
freeing and even an inspirational power.

Exercise

Relax and become still. Turn your attention inward. Breathe slowly and softly. Let thoughts just
pass through your mind without thinking them.

Simply remain in calmness. Then turn your attention to your particular avoidance. Don't think about it, evaluate it, or make judgments about it. Simply sit quietly and allow an image of it to form. Let any image come: of nature, an animal, or an artifact. Simply let the image come without attempting to guide it; let it unfold of itself. Don't specify what must come or how—whether you will see, hear, smell or intuit the image or feel it in your body. Just let any image present itself and form of its own nature. You may want to do this in the presence of Jesus and see him looking with you at the image of your avoidance.

When it seems right, you may want to write down what happened: any observations you may have about the particular way this image appeared and how it affected you.

APPENDIX II

Emotion Least Controlled

Each of the centers of the Enneagram personality study has an emotion least controlled. While all persons have open to them and can feel the full range of human emotion, there is a particular emotion with which one struggles during the whole of one's life. As long as these emotions are not dealt with they can be compulsive, tyranize the person and create havoc of all kinds. A psychologist would tell us: "Don't avoid them! Go through them! Bring them into the light and face them fairly and squarely. Only then will you be able to handle them." While the advice is sound, experience shows us that it is easier said than done. This is an area of darkness, an uncharted territory that could seemingly overwhelm us. Like Jesus, the earlier monks used to go out into the desert to battle the demons, trusting in God that they would conquer, "because you are from God and you have in you one who is greater than anyone in this world" (I Jn 4,4). It is with this kind of assurance that we invite persons to deal with the emotion of Fear, Anxiety and Anger in prayer. In this Appendix we will describe the emotion each center struggles to control and suggest prayer exercises which, hopefully, will open each to the transforming and healing love of God.

Head Center (Five-Six-Seven)
Least Controlled Emotion—Fear

Head centered people struggle with fear. Fear can be paralyzing and overwhelming for these persons. In listening to others they will realize that they are very often afraid when others are not; and even in situations where others experience fear, their own fear is more intense. These persons need to take the time to notice, to be in touch with the emotion within themselves. Noticing and naming an emotion is different from being overwhelmed by it. As a child I (John) had a great fear of the dark, and especially of the evil that lurked under my bed at night. With the encouragement of my parents I looked under the bed and realized that the feared monster, the bad person, was not there at all. When whatever we fear (even fear itself) is exposed to the light (the light of an understanding person, or especially God's light), it can be faced for what it really is. Fear that remains unfaced, or in the dark and unexposed, grows and can overwhelm us. The Psalmist was well aware that no darkness impedes the loving light of God.

> "If I asked darkness to cover me, and light to become night around me, that darkness would not be dark to you, night would be as light as the day." Ps 139, 1-2

Exercise

"Hear the Word of God in the Presence of God's love."

Take time to center yourself. Use the focus meditation which we discussed in chapter 4, if you wish. Relax and be still. Be aware of being in God's presence and listen to this word:

> "Courage! It is I! Do not be afraid." Mt 14,28
> "Do not be afraid; only have faith." Mk 5,37

> "Do not be afraid; for I have redeemed you; I have called you by your name, you are mine." Is 43,1

Let one of these verses sink deep within you. Repeat it aloud over and over. Allow yourself to let your fear surface (fear of emptiness, decisions, pain, sickness, or loneliness). Be with these fears before God and let God's word touch you as you are. You may want to express yourself in these or your own words:

> "Lord, here I am sitting with my fear. I do not know how to handle it. I place my life in your all loving hands. I open myself to your tender healing touch. I allow you to love me now."

Heart Center (Two-Three-Four)
Least Controlled Emotion—Anxiety

Heart Centered persons experience anxiety as the least controlled emotion.

It is helpful to distinguish anxiety from fear. These are two reactions to some perception of threat. In a fear response, a person's attention is drawn principally to the person, object or situation regarded as endangering one's well being, e.g., an assailant, a growling dog, a darkened house that one must enter alone. So fear reacts to a specific reality perceived as dangerous to one's well being and adjustment can be made to that object, person or thing. Anxiety, however, is a reaction to the perception of a threat that is vague. The feeling produced is one of diffuseness, uncertainty and helplessness before an unspecific danger. Anxiety is free floating, unattached to a specific object.

Heart centered people find themselves controlled by the outside world: its messages, directives and expectations. They live with a constant anxiety about meeting these.

Rollo May in *Man's Search for Himself*¹ points out that anxiety is a response to threats to one's existence or basic values. TWOS, THREES and FOURS find their security and values in being a helper (TWO), being successful (THREE) or being special (FOUR). This issue is prominent whether they are alone or in the presence of others. Being liked, accepted, approved of, recognized as a success, or as sensitive and refined are at stake in the everydayness of life.

Exercise

Take some time to relax and be still. Come before the presence of Jesus. Allow your anxiety to come to the surface of consciousness and sit with it as painful as it may be. (This will not be easy for heart centered persons because the world within appears as unknown and terrifying). Gradually learn to know and accept it in the presence of Jesus. Allow Jesus to walk into that anxiety and be with you there. Look together with him at the anxiety as he walks around the chambers of your heart. Look at him looking at you with love. Let him still the storm raging within you. Feel the anxiety lessen and its being lifted as a heavy weight from your heart. Rest in his presence, in his love.

Gradually your destructive, enervating anxiety can be befriended and turned into energy of compassionate concern for yourself and others. The process of befriending is gradual as God's love heals and transforms the emotion.

Gut Center (Eight-Nine-One)
Least Controlled Emotion—Anger

Gut centered persons find anger as the emotion with which they struggle. Anger can be readily expressed by the EIGHTS, but often in an excessive manner. NINES avoid this and other strong feelings by turning off the juice and so allow the anger to simmer and eventually reach the boiling point. ONES will avoid awareness of their anger and express it sideways in cutting remarks, being too nice, and projecting the evil outside them. In the past few years a lot of sound advice has been offered us by psychology about the need to recognize anger, get in touch with it, accept it and learn how to handle this powerful emotion.

Sound psychology can be helpful in this area. However, where anger is a particular difficulty as for gut centered persons, more than psychology is needed. Their anger needs healing, transformation and redemption. They need to yield themselves to the gracious and loving activity of God. Such a stance is not easy for persons in this center who strive to control reality: by power (EIGHT); by remaining settled (NINE); or by correcting reality (ONE).

In the experience of healing and transformation these persons will know something of the experience of the apostle Paul. We do not know whether his struggle in Romans 7 was with the emotion of anger, but gut centered persons know the difficulty that their willing something can be different from what they actually do.

> "For though the will to do what is good is in me, the performance is not, with the result that instead of doing the good things I want to do, I carry out the sinful things I do not want. When I act against my will, then, it is not my true self doing it, but sin which lives in me." Rm 7, 18-20

This certainly involved Paul in a deep emotional struggle in which he could not control reality simply by his own strength.

Exercise

Take some time to relax and be still. Perhaps use the centering way of silencing one's thoughts. Then simply sit quietly in the darkness in the presence of God. Try to get in touch with your anger and let it surface. Feel it within your body. Continue to stay deep within yourself where you meet God in the true self. You may then find yourself like a boat tossed in a storm. A storm may rage within you. Simply remain in the presence of the God who loves you and is within you—in this anger. Don't give up. Finally and gradually, you will triumph by the grace of God.

This prayer is a way of letting God transform our anger and employing it for God's reign and justice. Anger then will not be uncontrollable and overpowering. Rather as we befriend it, it will become a passion for holiness and justice. It is generally a step by step transformation but signs of growth will become perceptible, such as letting go of a hurt in forgiveness, an ability to stay with a conflict situation, or a capacity to tolerate patiently some imperfection. Along the way one will have the experience of praising and thanking God with St. Paul: "What a wretched man I am! Who will rescue me from this body doomed to death? Thanks be to God through Jesus Christ our Lord!" Rm 8, 24-25)

Other ways that the reader can work with the emotion least controlled is to engage it in dialogue or to image it as we discussed in Appendix I.

APPENDIX III

Kything Prayer[1] *And The Enneagram Personality Theory*

Kything is a form of spiritual connecting with other persons. It describes a center to center way of relating. Kything (or kithing) according to Webster means to make known or to become known. To kythe with another person is to make your true self, your heart, soul or center, present to the other. Your inner core becomes spiritually present to another person, without masks or disguises of any form.

The Scriptures speak profoundly of that form of spiritual presence and union. Jesus prayed:

> "May they all be one, Father, may they be one in us, as you are in me and I am in you, so that the world may believe it was you who sent me." Jn 17, 21

Such is the unfathomable unity of the Trinity. But also Jesus speaks of the union in grace of the believer with God:

> "If anyone loves me he will keep my word, and my Father will love him, and we shall come to him and make our home with him." Jn 14, 23

Loving and faithful responding to the Word means that the Father and Son would dwell in the person—a being at home with one another in grace; the believer and Christ would abide center to center in each other with completely open familiarity, like that of Father and Son. This is the experience St. Paul points to with his phrase "in Christ." Christ lives in Paul and Paul lives in him (Ga 2, 20). All the faithful too are in Christ and he prays that Christ may be in them: "May Christ live in your hearts through faith" (Ep 3, 17). This kind of connection at a deep level can also be found in the relationships between human persons and for this reason kything can be a valuable practice for persons when they are feeling compulsed or under some particular stress which seems overwhelming.

Kything is an activity that brings about a communion at the level of the spirit. It involves focusing your spiritual presence in another person or their presence in you. When we kythe with another person, at the level of the spirit with all of its energy and giftedness, we can share in their energies and giftedness.

Through the knowledge of the Enneagram we learn the Arrow Theory in which we discover that the way to health, wholeness or redemption is for each personality to MOVE AGAINST THE ARROW. So for the ONE wholeness comes in movement towards the SEVEN whose idealization is: "I am OK;" "I am fine." The SEVEN is optimistic, hopeful and joyful. In the fall of 1985 I, John, had to present the Enneagram program for the first time alone. I was mired prior to the weekend in a perfectionistic striving concerning all that I lacked in doing this and what

I should know, but might not. I drew strength at that time from a kything prayer with Barbara, who is a SEVEN, and her gifts and energy helped me become a bit more serene in approaching the weekend. The movement against the arrow is against one's own inclination and towards the health (for you) expressed by the idealization of the other personality (EIGHT towards the TWO; NINE towards the THREE; ONE towards the SEVEN; TWO towards the FOUR; THREE towards the SIX; FOUR towards the ONE: FIVE towards the EIGHT; SIX towards the NINE; SEVEN towards the FIVE).[2] We have found in our workshops that persons who have engaged in the kything prayer have been strengthened with the gift that they needed at the time.

In the kything prayer you want to choose someone who is close to you, and whom you trust, and to whom you can entrust yourself. You can choose someone who is in your good space (where you move to when moving against the arrow) and whose gifts you need. The person does not need to be physically present (Barbara was in Kenya when I kythed with her), nor need the person be living. We can kythe also with saints or with Jesus.

The kything prayer has four steps:

1) First become centered. Each of the centers may choose the path that suits them best. Once in touch with your inner self, then ask God to instill you and your kything partner with the divine spirit.

2) As soon as you are ready, let your center find itself within the person with whom you are kything. Your imagination can help you make the passage.

Picture yourself within the person, e.g., in their heart, standing or sitting beside the person, or being held or hugged by him/her. You want to do whatever is comfortable for you. At times in our workshop some people express uncomfortableness with entering into another's center, but could invite the other person's spirit into themselves. Do whatever is easy for you. Kything occurs in either form of union.

3) Invite the giftedness or energy you need to flow through your kything partner and into you. Be open to receive the gift or energy, and welcome them in quiet.

4) Thank God for the gifts and energy that come to you through the loving presence and communion with this other person. Ask God to bless and pour forth gifts, and energize those persons with whom you kythe. This is important because thankfulness is a response to the awareness that "everything is gift" and prayer needs to open out to express our care and concern for others.

ENNEAGRAM ARROW THEORY

In kything prayer, it can be very helpful to kythe with a person in your good space. The good space is identified through the theory of the arrows on the Enneagram.

Begin with your own number and go against the arrow that ends at your number. For example, if you are a FOUR, your bad space would be TWO while your good space is number ONE. The good space of NINE is THREE.

The bad space is named by flowing with the arrow.

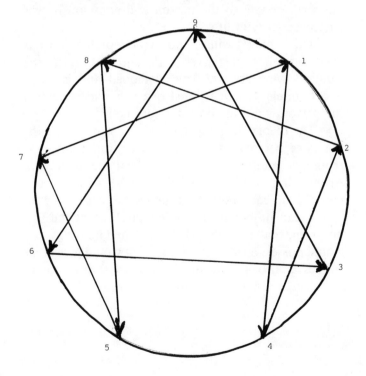

APPENDIX IV

Prayer With The Wings

The wings of an Enneagram personality are the numbers on either side of the number on the Enneagram circle. For example, the wings of ONE are TWO and NINE while the wings of SEVEN are SIX and EIGHT.

The wings are often labeled with the words "inner" and "outer." The "outer" wing is thought to be the stronger of the two, the one that somehow seemed more acceptable to the person and consciously was embraced early in life.

The "inner" wing is not as acceptable and has been critiqued negatively. Because of this, the "inner" wing remains less developed and is often poorly integrated. It is most often in evidence when the person is not in control emotionally.

The theory of the wings explains why persons of the same personality type may seem quite different from one another. A number FOUR could have a strong wing of either THREE or FIVE which would give a different emotional tone to the personality.

It can be noted in looking carefully at the Enneagram, that a number that integrated its wings well would possess a treasury of gifts that would give great fullness and beauty to the personality. For example, an EIGHT with a well developed SEVEN and NINE would certainly possess a balance that an EIGHT with a poorly developed "inner" wing could not claim.

The following prayer exercise is designed to help the pray-er to integrate more fully into his or her personality the giftedness of their "inner" wing.

Reflect on your own number and remember early life experiences. Were there qualities evident in your behavior that you felt good about and that are characteristic of one of your wings? For example, as a number SEVEN child, I, Barbara, can remember feeling very good about qualities of the SIX in myself while negatively critiquing the EIGHT characteristics. SIX is my "outer" wing and "EIGHT" is my inner wing.

Reflect on the qualities of your "inner wing." How do you feel about them? Most frequently people do not like them. It is this wing that is important to befriend and try to integrate in the interests of coming to greater balance and wholeness.

Prayer Exercise

Try to become centered using the methods described for your particular center.

In the presence of the Lord, let surface an image of your "inner" wing.

E.G.:

if NINE is the "inner" wing, a swing hanging loosely might be the image.

if SIX is the "inner" wing "goody two shoes" might be used.

if TWO is the "inner wing" a coffee pot might be the image.

Look at the image. Let God look at it with you. Be present to the feelings it evokes in you. Explore the feelings. Express them to God. Try to become comfortable with them in God's presence. What are they offering you in terms of insight about yourself?

Explore aspects of the image you have chosen. Walk around it. Look at it, its various parts. Hold it, touch it. What does it remind you of? Try to understand it and appreciate it. Speak to God about what you are finding. See what qualities it holds that are needed in your personality. What would you be like if you allowed the image to gift you?

Pray to accept and love these qualities and to let go of the resistance you might feel toward them. Ask God for the gift you need to be free of your resistances.

End with a prayer of gratitude. "I thank you God, for the wonder of my being," Ps 139:14.

This prayer exercise can be returned to over and over again with value as a person grows in wholeness.

APPENDIX V

Praying With Scripture

This appendix offers a number of scripture passages for each of the Enneagram personalities. The passages offered are divided into two sections for the respective number described.

The first section is entitled "Sinfulness to Pray Through" and the second "Giftedness to Rejoice in and Strengthen in Prayer." It is recommended that the passages be used as the individual person feels the need of a particular one. For example, when a number NINE is experiencing inertia that is leading to laziness, it would be important to stay with passages that touch that aspect of the NINE struggle. It is important to let the truth of God's message go deeper and deeper into one's mind and heart. "Sit with the passage" and don't move too quickly to another one. Let the chosen passage be like the waves of the shore washing gently over the disturbed sand of your being and restoring it gradually and gently to wholeness and beauty.

There are times when we are consciously rejoicing in our obvious giftedness. These are the times to use the giftedness passages in a spirit of loving gratitude to God. It is important in praying these passages to remember that our holiness and perfection is not a matter of attaining all possible virtue, but of coming to a greater fullness of that which is the particular giftedness of our own number.

You will note that some of the sinfulness and giftedness of a number seem to be contradictory. Remember that health in a number often brings a person to a kind of giftedness that is directly opposite the face of the struggle with which they are familiar.

These passages are by no means meant to be exhaustive. You may have others that are important to you and to which you have been naturally drawn over the years that you can now see as part of God's healing gift to you. You may discover other passages as you begin to focus your selections of scripture in the light of your knowledge of the Enneagram.

Scripture For Number Fives.

Sinfulness to pray through. . . .

' 1. FIVES suffer from a deep inner emptiness. Is 55: 1-3. Invitation to come to God to have the thirst of life quenched.

2. FIVES can remain on the outskirts of human life and are uninvolved. Lk 10:29-37. Parable of the Good Samaritan.

3. FIVES find any kind of active participation difficult. Is 52:7. How beautiful are the feet of those who bring good news.

4. FIVES hoard their wisdom. Jn 21: 15-17. If you love me, feed my lambs, sheep.

↘ 5. FIVES find it hard to articulate their insights, to concretize them. Jr 1:4-10. Do not be afraid. I am putting my words in your mouth.

• 6. FIVES can miss concrete details. Jn 21:1-14. Be aware of the level of awareness evident in so many areas in the passage.

7. FIVES never finish their preparation and never feel ready to come to closure. This keeps them out of active engagement in life. II Th 3:6-15. Work so as not to be a burden.

8. FIVES have no time boundaries and can be forever getting ready to work. Jn 9:4-5. There is an urgency about Jesus to work while He has time.

• 9. FIVES can become totally immersed in projects and miss other aspects of life. Mt 9:36-37. Witness Jesus' compassion for human need and his prayer that his apostles would respond to need.

10. FIVES question everything. Is 55:7-9. God's ways are not our ways. Live with mystery.

• 11. FIVES are critical. Jn 8:15-20. Danger of judging by human standards.

12. FIVES are over-objective and can forget people's feelings. Rm 14:17-21. God's work can be wrecked by being too objective.

• 13. FIVES lack tact. Truth is raw-boned. Ga 6:1-5. Set others right in a spirit of gentleness.

14. FIVES don't relate on the level of feelings. Jn 11:32-34. See Jesus deeply moved in a personal relationship.

15. FIVES can be distant, aloof and detached. I P 3:8-12. Rules for anyone who wants happiness.

16. FIVES are over observant. Lk 19:1-10. Jesus invites Zacchaeus to do more than look at him.

17. FIVES are cool. Ps 112. Prayer of the virtuous person who is involved in life.

18. FIVES lack an ability to make others comfor-

table with them. I P 4:7-11. Put yourselves at the service of others.

19. FIVES are stingy. I Tm 6:17-19. Be generous and willing to share.

20. FIVES compartmentalize. Col 2:6-8. Warning to not lose sight of the total mystery of Christ.

21. FIVES can show contempt. Jn 4. See the attitude of Jesus with the Samaritan woman.

22. FIVES are under loyal. Mt 9:27-31. Blind men disregard the stern warning of Jesus without regard to what that might mean for him.

23. FIVES are undercommitted. Mt 25: 31-46. Judgment is based on service to the neighbor.

24. FIVES resent being pushed. Gn 22: 1-19. Pray the blessings of Abraham's generosity.

25. FIVES are loners. Gn 2:18-24. It is not good for man to be alone, or woman either.

26. FIVES are easily embarrassed and ill at ease with others. Col 3:12-17. Called to be open and loving and in union with each other.

27. FIVES have a hard time asking for what they need. Mt 7:7-11. Ask and it will be given. At least begin to ask God.

28. FIVES are hoarders and miserly. Lk 21:1-4. Widow's mite. She gave all she had to live on.

29. FIVES hang on to the past. Ez 36:25-29. God's forgiveness and the creation of a new heart.

30. FIVES are extremely protective of themselves. Jn 12: 24-28. Unless the grain of wheat falls to the ground and dies.

31. FIVES procrastinate until they know exactly what to do. Qo 11:1-6. Cast your bread upon the waters.

32. FIVES are takers. Ac 20:35. There is more happiness in giving than in receiving.

Giftedness to be rejoiced in and prayed through. . .

1. FIVES are open minded. Col 2:1-5. Paul's desire to teach the mystery of Christ.

2. FIVES are receptive to new facts. Ep 4:21-24. The spiritual revolution.

3. FIVES are curious. Jn 3:1-21. Conversation of Jesus with Nicodemus.

4. FIVES are objective. Ac 15:7-12. Peter's understanding of God's ways of viewing life.

5. FIVES love to learn. Ps 119:33-4. A prayer to know God's ways.

6. FIVES are original thinkers. I Cor 1:17-31. True and false wisdom.

7. FIVES are provocative. Jr 16:1-13. Quality and style of Jeremiah's life is provocative.

8. FIVES are deep. Rm 11:33-36. Depths of God's wisdom and knowledge.

9. FIVES can move others to new ways of thinking. Ac 22: 1-21. Bearing witness by Paul to his new ways of believing and the gift of his conversion.

10. FIVES are wise. Si 51:13-22. Poem on the quest for wisdom.

11. FIVES have an inner power and strength. Ep 3:14-21. Prayer to grasp God's love more deeply.

12. FIVES are patient. Jm 5:7-11. Be patient as the farmer.

13. FIVES are comfortable with process. Mk 4:26-29. Seed growing by itself.

14. FIVES are sympathetic. Ph 2:1-5. Have

tenderness and sympathy.

15. FIVES sense patterns and see the broad picture. Jn 9:1-41. Cure of the man born blind. Jesus sees the perspective that is missed by the Jews.

16. FIVES are gentle and non-threatening. Is 49:15-16. The gentle, motherly love of God.

17. FIVES have clarity of vision. Ep 4:14-16. Don't be carried along by every wind of doctrine.

18. FIVES are thorough. 2 Tm 4: 1-5. Solemn charge to Timothy to be thorough in his service of the word.

19. FIVES are organizers. Pr 16:1-33. God's guidance in human planning.

20. FIVES are excellent listeners. Qo 5:1-6. Don't be in a hurry to speak.

21. FIVES have a gift of discernment that comes from seeing through things. I Jn 4:1-3. Test the spirits.

SCRIPTURE FOR NUMBER SIX

Sinfulness to be prayed through. . .

1. SIXES feel unconnected with the stream of life. I Cor 12:1-30. Interconnectedness of the parts of the body.

2. SIXES over-emphasize authority in their effort to make connections. Mt 20:24-28. Among the pagans there is need to make authority felt.

3. SIXES are fearful people. Mt 10:26-33. Do not be afraid.

4. SIXES are plagued by uncertainty and doubt. They have no tolerance for ambiguity. Jn 16:13-15. The Spirit will lead you to complete truth.

5. SIXES withdraw to get their position. Lk 24: 44-49. Stay in the city until you are clothed with power from God.

6. SIXES envy others' ability to deal with feelings and decisions. Jn 11:32-41. Pray to feel and decide as Jesus does.

7. SIXES are inhibited. Heb 4:14-16. Be confident in approaching God.

8. SIXES are cautious and overly prudent. Rm 8:26-27. Spirit comes to help us in our weakness.

9. SIXES are indecisive and blocked in action. 2 Th 3:1-5. The fortitude Christ gives.

10. SIXES need to check everything out. Jn 16:5-15. Power of the Spirit will critique human judgment.

11. SIXES are distrustful. I P 2:1-3. Integrity in relationships.

13. SIXES vacillate. Lk 11:23. He/She who is not with me is against me.

14. SIXES are overly shy. Jn 15:26-27. Power of the Spirit in human life.

15. SIXES are overly anxious. Is 41:10-11. Stop being anxious, I will give you strength.

16. SIXES can be dogmatic. Mt 23:8-12. You have only one teacher.

17. SIXES are willing to give up their independence for inclusion and security. Ac 4:18-22. Courage of Peter and John before the Sanhedrin.

18. SIXES are dependent persons. Col 2:6-8. Be rooted in Christ, let no one deprive you of freedom.

19. SIXES over-stress fidelity to laws. Ph 3:6-16. Paul is no longer seeking the perfection that comes from the law. It led him to persecute Christ.

20. SIXES are legalistic. Col 2:16-23. Growing in Christ to the point of not letting others dictate one's conduct.

21. SIXES are pharisaical. They place burdens on others. Mt 23:13-32. Indictment of the Scribes and Pharisees.

22. SIXES need to justify themselves and seek other's justification. I Cor 2:1-5. Paul can only rely on the power of the Spirit.

23. SIXES are very aware of who is on their side and who is against them. I Cor 3:5-9. Apollos and Paul are only human. God is the important person.

24. SIXES are hesitant and unsure. I Cor 16:13-14. Stand firm in faith. Be brave and strong.

25. SIXES are nervous and jerky. I P 5:5-11. Be calm and vigilant.

26. SIXES are blind to their own deviance and project it onto others. Jn 12: 1-11. Judas is blind to his own deceit.

27. SIXES are secretive. I Jn 1:5-7. Walk in the light.

28. SIXES have difficulty asking for what they need. Lk 11:9-13. Ask and it will be given to you.

29. SIXES are overly serious. Jn 17:21-23. Jesus prays for his disciples and expresses the wish to share his glory with them even in the face of his death.

30. SIXES can be defiant. Jon 1:1-16. Jonah rebells against his mission.

31. SIXES can be resentful. Jon 4:1-11. God's answer to Jonah's resentment.

Giftedness to rejoice in and to pray with. . . .

1. SIXES are cooperative. Mt 22:15-22. Render to Caesar what is Caesar's.

2. SIXES are reciprocal in relationships. Rm 12:3-13. Do not exaggerate your own importance.

3. SIXES enter into warm-hearted friendships marked by deep emotion and feeling. Jn 20:11-18. Mary's warm, passionate love for Jesus.

4. SIXES are whimsical and tease those they like. They can be stimulating and fun. Lk 2:39-40. Go to Nazareth and look in on the relationships in the household.

5. SIXES are faithful. Ep 6:10-20. Grow strong in the Lord.

6. SIXES are constant. Lk 6:46-49. Build your house upon a rock.

7. SIXES protect those they love. Rm 15:1-6. The strong have the duty to put up with those who are weak.

8. SIXES can be innovators in leadership and see new possibilities. Lk 6:1-5. Jesus sees the need to critique the laws of the Sabbath.

9. SIXES respect tradition. Mt 5:17-19. Jesus does not come to abolish the law, but to bring it to fullness.

10. SIXES have foresight and courage. 2 Tm 1:6-14. God's gift is not a spirit of timidity.

11. SIXES are loyal. Lk 24:13-35. Jesus continues to be concerned about his disciples.

12. SIXES are good parenting types. Mt 19:13-15. Jesus' love for the children.

13. SIXES foster growth in others. Lk 19:11-27. Parable of the pounds.

14. SIXES are responsible people. 2 Cor 4:1-6.

We have a work entrusted to us. There must be no weakening.

15. SIXES are gracious hosts and hostesses. Lk 22:14-18. The meal is his most important forum.

16. SIXES do not leave a lot of things hanging. They are single-minded. 2 Tm 4:1-5. Keep orientation clear.

17. SIXES are balanced in relationships. 2 Tm 2:22-26. Call to a balanced way of relating.

18. SIXES are approachable. Mt 11:28-30. Come to me.

19. SIXES are compassionate. Mt 18:12-14. Lost sheep. The individual is important and felt for.

20. SIXES are prudent. 2 Tm 3:14-17. Keep to what you have been taught. Do not go after fads.

21. SIXES reverence and learn from elders. Heb 12:1-4. Strength of the witness of our ancestors in the faith.

SCRIPTURE FOR NUMBER SEVEN

Sinfulness to Pray Through . . .

1. SEVENS over-idealize. Si 2. Be prepared for difficulties.

2. SEVENS tend to withdraw when they are hurt. Heb 2:5-18. Jesus remaining in the painful human reality and submitting to death.

3. SEVENS live in the future to avoid the pain of the present. II Cor 1:3-7. Be present to the God of consolation.

4. SEVENS don't deal with pain of the past. They move on too quickly and fail to learn the lessons

pain can teach them. Heb 5:7-10. What Jesus learned in pain.

5. SEVENS are daydreamers. Lk 13:6-9. The need to bear fruit.

6. SEVENS move to new things too quickly. Mk 7:24-30. Perseverance of the Syrophoenician woman.

7. SEVENS' plans can be abstract and unrealistic. Jr 29:11-14. Try to get in touch with God's plans for the future and the people.

8. SEVENS find it hard to make concrete decisions to fulfill their plans. Dt 30:15-20. The call to choose.

9. SEVENS are poor on the carry through. Their enthusiasm can die too quickly. Lk 14:34-35. Salt losing its savor.

10. SEVENS are impractical and need to learn how to take concrete steps to fulfill their plans. Mk 9:2-8. Transfiguration. Peter wants to stay and cease his engagement in real life.

11. SEVENS can have abstract visions that do not get put into practice or are out of touch with reality. Mt 7: 21-27. A call to do the will of God, not just think about it.

12. SEVENS can be insensitive in the ways they impose their plans on others. 2 Cor 1:15-2:4. Paul changes his plans because of his sensitivity to his situation.

13. SEVENS can be naive. Ps 62. Put your trust in God not in human beings.

14. SEVENS avoid what is painful, disruptive, or negative. Jr 18: 1-18. See what the potter is capable of doing with what was originally not good.

15. SEVENS can be superficial and tend to keep

things light. Ws 9:9-18. Prayer for wisdom and depth.

16. SEVENS repress or project pain and do not learn its lessons. Ph 2:6-11. See Jesus enter into pain and death.

17. SEVENS can wear a compulsive smile and not let others see their real feelings. Ho 2:14-20. A call to go into the desert. It is the place where the SEVENS will come to the truth about themselves and God.

18. SEVENS can have a Pollyanna attitude. Mk 8:31-33. Peter's response to the prediction of the passion.

19. SEVENS rationalize to maintain themselves in a heavy world. Mk 14:32-42. See Jesus struggle to face his passion, but his willingness to do it.

20. SEVENS can be self deceptive. Lk 22:31-34. Peter's "out-of-touchness" with his own weakness.

21. SEVENS struggle with the sin of gluttony and take too much of what is good to reduce the pain of life. Mt 6:19-21. Do not lay up treasures.

22. SEVENS are talkative and can gossip. Jm 3:1-12. Control of tongue.

23. SEVENS have a demanding quality about them. They want an immediate response. Lk 16:1-8. The crafty steward makes demands on others he himself could not meet.

24. SEVENS would like someone to care for them and their needs, but they find it hard to listen to others' problems. Mt 7:12. Golden Rule.

25. SEVENS can be angry, volatile and vindictive if they are cornered. Jm 4:1-3. Anger that comes from having plans frustrated.

26. SEVENS do for people to gain their friend-

ship. Lk 17:7-10. We have done no more than our duty.

27. SEVENS find it hard to confront, to be "un-nice." Mt 10:34-36. Jesus is a cause of dissension.

28. SEVENS find it difficult to stay in a discussion that gets heavy and will move away either physically or by lightening it. Lk 12:51-53. Expect difficulties.

29. SEVENS are impatient. Mt 13:24-30. Parable of the darnel. Don't move too quickly.

30. SEVENS can be flighty and over-active. Ps 46:10. Be still and know that I am God.

31. SEVENS are careful about the level at which they give themselves. Mk 12:41-44. Widow's mite. SEVENS often give only of the superfluous of their lives and don't share deeply or become vulnerable.

Giftedness to rejoice in and to pray through . . .

1. SEVENS are appreciative. Lk 1:46-55. Awareness of the graciousness of God.

2. SEVENS are most joyous of the numbers. Ph 4:4. Paul expresses his deep appreciation for Christian joy.

3. SEVENS see giftedness in everything and delight in life and in nature. Ps 104. Beauties of the world.

4. SEVENS are aware of surfaces and sensations. There is a sense of the immediate in them. Lk 5:12-16. Cure of the leper involves the sensitive act of touching.

5. SEVENS are sensitive to others. Mk 2:1-12. Cure of the paralytic. Jesus is sensitive to the deeper, unspoken need for forgiveness in the man.

6. SEVENS come to a sense there is enough of everything and nothing is superfluous. Ps 23. I shall not want. You prepare a banquet before me.

7. SEVENS can be content without demanding more. Ps 131. My heart has no lofty ambitions.

8. SEVENS celebrate life. Col 3:16-17. With gratitude in your heart sing to God.

9. SEVENS have a sense of the communion among persons and things. Ps 133. How good it is for all to live in harmony.

10. SEVENS are visionary about the future. Rm 8:18-27. Glory is our destiny.

11. SEVENS are capable of communicating enthusiasm and inspiring others to follow them. Is 52:7-12. The joy of bringing the good news.

12. SEVENS are childlike. Mt 11:25-27. The revelation of the good news to the childlike.

13. SEVENS are optimistic. Col 1:3-14. Confident reliance on God's power to save.

14. SEVENS see possibilities. They have an inner vision of how things will work. Is 42:10-17. Hymn of triumph.

15. SEVENS are friendly and outgoing. Lk 5:29-32. Imagine Jesus at this party.

16. SEVENS like to make others happy. Jn 12:1-11. Mary wants to do for Jesus. The sensitive gesture.

17. SEVENS have the gift of humor. Lk 19:1-10. Zacchaeus in the tree. Just look at the scene and enjoy it with Jesus.

18. SEVENS are good at entertaining and are hospitable. Jn 1:35-39. Be with Jesus and the disciples as they spend the day together.

19. SEVENS have a natural simplicity. Ps 101. Purity of heart praised.

20. SEVENS are practical and resourceful. Pr 31:10-31. The ideal wife, her virtues.

21. SEVENS are playful. Zp 3:14-17. Rejoice and dance with God.

22. SEVENS are very hope-filled persons. Ps 27. God is my light and my salvation.

SCRIPTURE FOR THE NUMBER TWO

Sinfulness to Pray Through . . .

＼ 1. TWOS experience an inner emptiness that can lead them away from attending to themselves and avoid the inner journey by reaching out. Ps 103. Faces them with God's loving acceptance of their frailty.

2. TWOS see themselves as full of inadequacy and others as more worthy of attention. Lk 1: 5-25. Zechariah's disbelief of God's graciousness to him.

＊ 3. TWOS often give out of a need to feel good about themselves. Lk 17:7-10. A call to humble, simple giving for the right reasons.

4. TWOS feel they will be liked only if they give. Their identity is tied into their giving. Rm 12: 3-13. Speaks of the humility and charity which should mark all giving.

5. TWOS find it hard to receive. Jn 13: 1-16. Let Jesus wash your feet. How does it feel?

• 6. TWOS can be aggressive in relationships. Jn 6: 59-71. Jesus' freedom in letting others come or go.

7. TWOS can be controlling. 1 Th 5: 19-22. Never suppress the Spirit. Think before you act.

, 8. TWOS can feel unappreciated and misunderstood. 2 Th 3:13. Never tire of doing good.

• 9. TWOS deal with a lot of unowned anger. Their world view includes the expectation that all should be caring for and protecting others. 1 Th 5: 14-18. Be patient with the weak who do not see what you see.

• 10. TWOS feel guilty that they have needs. Mt 26: 36-46. Jesus showed his need and fear to his disciples and asked for their support.

• 11. TWOS are self-sufficient. 1 S 2: 1-10. Prayer of Hannah. She recognized her need for God.

12. TWOS lack genuine warmth. Mk 5: 35-43. The genuine warmth of Jesus with the little girl.

13. TWOS find intimacy difficult. Everyone is their friend. Jn 14:23-31. Describes Jesus' intimate sharing of himself with those closest to him, his disciples.

14. TWOS are flatterers. Pr 29:5. The flatterer sets a net for another's feet.

• 15. TWOS are advice givers. Col 3: 16-17. Advice should only be given when the message of God has found a home within the person.

16. TWOS do not always follow through on their promises. 2 Cor 7: 1-4. Reflect on what it means to have a basis for hope, to know that promises made will be fulfilled.

, 17. TWOS can have a "martyr complex." Rm 15: 1-6. All are called to put up with difficulties.

• 18. TWOS resent time taken from them. Mk 1: 32-34. Even after sunset crowds came to Jesus to be healed.

19. TWOS know what it is to be anxious. Mt 6: 25-34. Trust in providence.

20. TWOS sometimes become overwhelmed by all their giving. Lk 10: 38-42. Martha became overwhelmed by all the serving.

· 21. TWOS can become hysterical in crises. Mk 4: 35-41. The storm at sea is a call to trust in the turbulent times.

22. TWOS can be superficial and joke at times that are serious. Lk 8: 49-56. The crowds laughed at Jesus not realizing his power.

23. TWOS are possessive and try to protect persons they help from others. Jn 17: 6-11. Jesus recognized that the disciples did not belong to him.

24. TWOS sometimes scorn persons who are "too introspective." They tend to overemphasize the practical to the detriment of the interior. Jn 12: 1-11. In the anointing at Bethany, Judas' concern for the practical caused him to miss the depth reality present.

· 25. TWOS are often stranger to their own feelings and don't know what is going on inside of them. Ps 139. Let God look at them and know their heart.

26. TWOS can be manipulative. Mk 3: 20-21. Relatives try to rescue Jesus.

· 27. TWOS idealize love and sentimentality. 1 Jn 3: 18-20. Our love is not just to be mere talk.

28. TWOS rescue others in conversation and soothe them. Jm 3: 13-18. Show your wisdom not in words, but in humility and good example.

29. TWOS most often are unable to get directly angry. Mk 8: 31-33. Jesus challenges Peter spontaneously and directly.

30. TWOS have a false humility and put

themselves down. Ez 34: 11-16. God's goodness to all kinds of people.

◆ 31. TWOS find it extraordinarily difficult to handle rejection. Lk 4: 16-30. Rejection of Jesus at Nazareth.

◆ 32. TWOS are ambitious. Mk 10: 35-40. Sons of Zebedee go after the best seats!

◆ 33. TWOS are always available. They cannot set limits or say no. Mk 1: 35. See Jesus setting prayer structures for himself.

Giftedness to Rejoice In And Strengthen In Prayer . . .

◆ 1. TWOS are very aware of others' needs in the concrete world of health, education, and sustenance. Mk 5: 25-34. An on-the-way cure coming out of Jesus' heightened awareness of human need.

◆ 2. TWOS are considerate of the feelings of others. Ac 9: 26-30. Barnabas' role in introducing Paul to the apostles who were afraid of him.

◆ 3. TWOS express appreciation of others. Rm 1: 8-15. Paul's Thanksgiving.

◆ 4. TWOS possess a free and generous spirit of sharing. Mk 9: 41. Giving a cup of cold water.

◆ 5. TWOS have an innate gift of responding thoughtfully. Mk 10: 46-52. Cure of Bartimaeus.

◆ 6. TWOS nurture others. Ph 4: 10-20. Paul's gratitude for the support he has received.

◆ 7. TWOS are loyal to those in pain and are aware of the "underdog." Rm 8: 31-39. Fidelity of God's love.

◆ 8. TWOS are sensitive. Col 4: 5-6. Tact and sensitivity are encouraged.

· 9. TWOS are selfless. Mk 6: 30-34. Jesus' willingness to put off rest to respond to need.

· 10. TWOS are empathetic. Mk 1: 29-31. Cure of Peter's mother-in-law.

11. TWOS are gentle and non-threatening. Mk 10: 13-16. Jesus and the children.

· 12. TWOS are responsible. Mt 26: 17-19. Speaks of making preparations and attending to detail.

13. TWOS can listen with the heart. Lk 23: 39-43. Jesus even in his pain listened deeply to the prayer of the good thief.

· 14. TWOS are orientated toward the individual. Lk 19: 1-10. Jesus notices Zacchaeus in the crowd.

15. TWOS are really loving persons. Mt 20: 1-16. Shows the ability to respond to need not just what is deserved.

· 16. TWOS are appreciative. Lk 7: 1-10. Jesus appreciates the faith of the centurion.

· 17. TWOS are supportive. Mk 6: 45-52. Jesus walking on the water to comfort his apostles.

18. TWOS love the world. Jn 3: 16. God so loved the world.

· 19. TWOS can grow to have less need to be the center of giving. Lk 14: 7-11. Taking a lower place.

· 20. TWOS are very aware of the emotional atmosphere around them. Mt 20: 24-28. Jesus is aware of the strain among his disciples and responds objectively to it in a teaching.

· 21. TWOS have a genuine compassion. Lk 6: 36-38. A call to compassion and generosity.

SCRIPTURE FOR THE NUMBER THREE

Sinfulness To Pray Through . . .

1. THREES are overly concerned with being successful. Mk 6: 1-6. Jesus is rejected at Nazareth.

2. THREES make great efforts to unite with other persons but still often feel separate. Ep 4: 1-6. A call to unity at the deepest level.

3. THREES can feel inadequate and incapable when they are not succeeding. Is 30: 15-18. A call to trust in the gracious God.

4. THREES tend to view any failure as a personal failure. Lk 19: 41-44. Jesus weeps over Jerusalem's unbelief.

5. THREES spend too much energy and time in the outer world rather than in the inner world. Ep 3: 14-21. Paul prays for the hidden self to grow strong.

6. THREES give an overemphasis to roles and jobs and define themselves by them. Mk 9: 33-37. Jesus responds to the desire of the disciples to be the greatest with the servant saying and the image of the child.

7. THREES have an underdeveloped interior life. They feel a lack of confidence and knowledge in this area. Ez 11: 17-21. God gives a heart of flesh to replace a heart of stone.

8. THREES are fearful of the unknown world within them and of inner demons. Mk 7: 14-23. Jesus declares that what comes from inside makes a person unclean.

9. THREES deal with a lot of anxiety. Ps 62. Hope in God alone.

10. THREES tend to brag about their accomplishments, what they have done or whom they have influenced. Lk 17: 7-10. Jesus speaks of the attitude of humble service.

11. THREES put too much importance on degrees, memberships and titles. Jn 15: 9-17. God and Jesus' love, and love for one another are proclaimed by Jesus.

12. THREES are not always accurate and honest in speech because of the need to sell themselves or the product. Jn 3: 17-21. A call to live by and do the truth.

13. THREES can view everything in terms of the utilitarian. They gain knowledge for the sake of doing. Ph 4: 6-9. The good, noble, true and pure are values to be treasured.

14. THREES can allow their plans to become more important than people. Rm 13: 8-10. Love sums up the commandments of the Law.

15. THREES can behave as not quite present to people in relationships. Rm 12: 9-10. Love without pretence.

16. THREES can be quite superficial. Jr 31: 33-34. The new covenant is interior.

17. THREES tend to be abrupt. Mk 10: 13-16. Jesus, unlike the disciples, can waste time and bless the children.

18. THREES are aggressive. Mt 11: 28-30. Presents Jesus as gentle and humble in heart.

19. THREES can be angry at the inefficiency and incompetence of others. Ex 34: 6-7. Presents God's patience, long suffering and kindness with stubborn Israel.

20. THREES tend to decide quickly without sufficient concern for the consequences. Mk 6: 17-29. The beheading of John the Baptist. Herod made a hasty promise which he regretted to Herodias' daughter.

21. THREES can jump ship when the organization or project seems to be sinking. Jn 6: 67-71. Some left Jesus after the Discourse on Bread. He asks: "Do you want to go away too?" This faces them with the question of loyalty.

22. THREES don't learn from the past. As they don't admit mistakes, they don't learn from them. 1 Cor 10: 1-13. Warns them that Israel failed to learn from its mistakes. God will always provide the strength for the trial.

23. THREES can name their feelings but don't deal with them. Mk 4: 35-41. Jesus calms the storm. This passage invites them to ask Jesus to be with them in the inner storm.

24. THREES find it hard to be vulnerable because they need to keep up the image. 1 Cor 1: 26-2, 5. God chose the weak as followers. Paul was not afraid to express his own weakness.

25. THREES are competitive. Mt 23: 8-12. Jesus tells the disciples not to claim titles such as rabbi or teacher, but simply to glory in being a servant.

26. THREES have no private selves, but simply public faces. Jn 14: 23. Says that God desires to dwell within them.

27. THREES are vain. Mt 23: 5-7. Jesus criticizes the outward display of the scribes and the pharisees.

28. THREES have pseudo-feelings. Jn 11: 32-38. Jesus' weeping at the death of Lazarus, his friend, challenges them.

29. THREES can simulate the feelings which would be appropriate for the occasion and also can exaggerate. Rm 12: 15. Calls them to have a real empathy with others.

30. THREES can be manipulative and lobby for their position or stance. Lk 22: 24-27. Jesus responds to the disciples' desire to be the greatest, which they discussed at the Last Supper, with a servant saying.

31. THREES can be cold with inefficient people. Mk 12: 41-44. Confronts them with a Jesus who contemplates the widow who gave the mite.

32. THREES can make even prayer an achievement and highly organize it. Rm 8: 26-27. Reminds them that the Spirit is the source of our prayer and is present in the midst of our weakness.

33. THREES will argue a topic and find themselves unable to admit that they don't know something. Lk 6: 39. Relates the Parable of the blind guide.

Giftedness To Rejoice In And Strengthen In Prayer. . .

1. THREES have confidence. Ps 131. Invites to a childlike trust in God.

2. THREES are self assured and popular personalities. They know how to be "in." I Jn 4: 7-10. Grounds this in God's love.

3. THREES are community builders. Ep 4: 7-16. Calls to build the Body of Christ.

4. THREES get things done, finish the task. Mt 14: 13-21. They can ponder Jesus feeding the crowd with bread.

5. THREES are able to set personal goals and make decisions quickly. Mt 9: 35-10:1. Jesus feels the

distress of the crowds and sends out the Twelve.

6. THREES can facilitate others in their setting of goals. Ph 1: 3-11. Paul's Thanksgiving and Prayer out of his heart invites them to even deeper connectedness with others.

7. THREES have instinctive gifts of appraising tasks and knowing the direction of movements. Lk 6: 12-16. Shows Jesus choosing the Twelve out of a context of prayer. This context too would deepen their gift.

8. THREES are able to articulate easily. Jm 1: 22-25. Challenges with the image of the mirror a listening to the Word and acting upon it. Words are not enough.

9. THREES, who are in touch with themselves, present to their inner world, are able to be sensitively present to others and caring. Lk 7: 36-50. Jesus shows great sensitivity in forgiving the woman who was a sinner.

10. THREES possess great organizational ability and make good administrators. Lk 12: 35-48. The parable and sayings on being a faithful servant encourage them to a responsible use of their gift.

11. THREES see life in terms of connecting and belonging. The group and its destiny are important to them. Jn 17. Containing Jesus' prayer for the community of disciples can strengthen this disposition.

12. THREES have a power of persuasion that can influence others. Jn 1: 35-39. This call of the two disciples invites them to contemplate the attractiveness and persuasiveness of Jesus.

13. THREES have a capacity to facilitate the interaction of people. Lk 14: 12-14. Speaks about choosing guests to invite to a dinner. It challenges

them to be attentive to the seemingly unimportant persons with their gifts.

14. THREES are energetic. 1 Cor 3: 5-9. Reminds them that it is God who is working through them.

15. THREES can be a positive force for building up any area with which they are connected and are efficient. Lk 19: 1-10. Jesus brings salvation to the house of Zacchaeus, the tax collector. The story can invite them to allow his transforming presence into their inner world.

16. THREES are enthusiastic. Mt 12: 33-37. Words reveal the quality of the heart. The sayings remind them that good things come from inner goodness.

17. THREES are pragmatic and sensate. Lk 16: 1-8. The Parable of the crafty steward reminds them to use their pragmatic sense in the service of God's values.

18. THREES are available and generous. 1 Cor 13. Describes the quality of love.

19. THREES have the capacity to delegate. They can turn over the responsibility until the thing is required. Ac 6: 1-7. Shows the apostles delegating the appointment of the seven who would serve at table, while they continued the ministry of the word.

20. THREES know how to economize with money and time. Ga 6: 7-10. Speaks of the benefit of living in the Spirit and encourages not to grow tired of doing good.

SCRIPTURE FOR NUMBER FOUR

Sinfulness to Pray Through . . .

1. FOURS are dissatisfied. Lk 24: 13-35.

Disciples on the road to Emmaus. Jesus can enter into their disappointment.

2. FOURS can't be ordinary or natural. Mk 10:13-16. Children found Jesus easy to be with.

3. FOURS romanticize feeling. Mt 5:37. Jesus calls to simplicity of expression.

4. FOURS lack joy. Phil 4:4-9. Be happy, always happy in the Lord.

5. FOURS are envious. Jm 4:1-3. Envy is a source of disunity and leads to fights and battles.

6. FOURS are complainers. Jon 4. The prophet complains. God answers.

7. FOURS hold on to hurts and pain. Mk 10:46-52. Eagerness of Bartimaeus to be free of his suffering and Jesus' response.

8. FOURS are inadaptable. Mt 15:21-28. Cure of the daughter of the Canaanite woman. Jesus adapts his mission to reach out to this non-Israelite.

9. FOURS are aloof, disdaining, snobbish. Col 3:12-15. Rules for Christian behavior include kindness, gentleness, patience and bearing with one another.

10. FOURS are elitist and don't relate easily with the common clay. Mt 9:9-13. Call of Matthew and eating with sinners. Tax collectors and sinners are very comfortable with Jesus.

11. FOURS entertain an elaborate fantasy life. It keeps them out of touch with reality. Lk 9:28-36. Transfiguration. Peter wants to continue the experience; Jesus invites him into the crowd.

12. FOURS are not comfortable with themselves. Is 43:1-5. God calls them by name and finds them precious.

13. FOURS are serious and seem never to find real happiness. Lk 19:1-10. See Jesus with Zacchaeus and notice his delighted response.

14. FOURS are preoccupied with death which they dread. Lk 10:29-37. Good Samaritan. FOURS need to reach out to others in need in order to overcome their darkness.

15. FOURS are depressed. Ps 22. Prayer of Jesus on the cross. Notice how his honest naming of his pain and struggle ended in thanksgiving.

16. FOURS talk when out of control. Col 4:5-6. Recommendations on acceptable speech.

17. FOURS play roles and are on stage most of the time. Mt 23:8-12. Jesus warns against playing roles such as Rabbi and Teacher.

18. FOURS are self-centered. I Jn 3:16-20. Love is real and active.

19. FOURS try to control their environment. Mk 8:27-33. Peter confronts Jesus and tries to control the mission.

20. FOURS have expectations for their friends and are not loyal if others don't conform. Lk 22:31-34. Jesus prays for Peter and remains faithful to one who denies him.

21. FOURS lack spontaneity. Mk 1:40-45. Cure of the leper. Look at the natural responses and feelings of Jesus.

22. FOURS are removed from the messy work and resist it. Qo 3:1-8. There is a season for everything in the human condition.

23. FOURS are brittle; there is no flow in their lives. Jm 5:7-11. Be in tune with the normal process of life.

24. FOURS are over analytical. Jb 38-39. Job bows to the wisdom of God which is beyond human understanding.

25. FOURS find it hard to relate to a group. Mk 6:30-44. Jesus lets go of his own needs to be with the crowd in its need.

26. FOURS are over sensitive to rejection. Jn 18:33-40. Jesus before Pilate. See his experience and response to rejection.

27. FOURS are loners. Gn 2:18-24. God says it is not good for man to be alone or woman either!

28. FOURS are unforgiving. Mt 18:21-35. Seventy times seven you must forgive. Forgiveness is the condition for a relationship with God.

Giftedness to rejoice in and strengthen in prayer . . .

1. FOURS appreciate and foster beauty in the world around them. Si 43:13-37. Delight in the wonders of nature.

2. FOURS are sensitive to the outer world. Lk 10:23-24. Happy are those who have seen and heard what you have seen and heard.

3. FOURS have the gift of expressing themselves artistically. Lk 1:67-79. Zechariah's beautiful expressing of God's gifting in the Benedictus.

4. FOURS are sensitive to people. Jn 2:1-12. Mary's sensitivity at Cana.

5. FOURS are in touch with the energy of life. I Jn 1:1-4. Be present to the experience of Jesus and its power.

6. FOURS are natural ecumenists. Ac 10:34-36.

Anyone of any nationality who fears God is acceptable to Him/Her.

7. FOURS do not separate the sacred and the secular. All is sacred. I Jn 4:1-3. Ability to recognize the Spirit in human life.

8. FOURS are at home in the world of the unconscious. Rm 8:1-13. Life in the Spirit.

9. FOURS are refined and cultured. Ep 4:25-32. The importance of respecting one another.

10. FOURS are creative and imaginative persons. Jr 18:1-12. Potter's artistic and creative gift.

11. FOURS are good-mannered. Ep 4:1-6. Live a life worthy of your call.

12. FOURS are deep. I Cor 2:10-14. Depths of God in the human spirit.

13. FOURS are sensitive to the emotional tone of a group. Jn 13:1-16. Sensitivity of Jesus to the feelings of his disciples in the scene.

14. FOURS have the capacity to change painful experiences of life into something beautiful. 2 Cor 4:16-18. The outer body is decaying, the inner is being renewed.

15. FOURS bring themselves to what they are doing. They become involved in the present. I Cor 3:10-17. You must work carefully.

16. FOURS are very generous when asked to spend themselves on a project. They do it well. Is 6:1-9. Isaiah's willingness to serve.

17. FOURS recognize others' talents. I Cor 10:31-33. I try to be helpful to everyone. I do not look only for my own advantage.

18. FOURS can appreciate the ordinary and simple things of life. Ps 8. I see your heavens, moon and stars.

SCRIPTURE FOR THE NUMBER EIGHT

Sinfulness To Pray Through . . .

1. EIGHTS look to see who has the power and gravitate toward it. 2 Cor 5:14. Pray to let the love of Christ control them and not an image of power that is strictly human control.

2. EIGHTS are acutely aware of their own power and can use it to bully or intimidate others. Lk 9:51-56. The apostles want to send down fire and destroy a city. Jesus teaches them. The EIGHTS need to listen carefully to the words of Jesus.

3. EIGHTS have a great sensitivity to their own hearts. Lk 6:27-38. The passage intimates that we are all hurt and are all called to love our enemies. The kind of forgiveness spoken of in this passage is the height of virtue for an EIGHT.

4. EIGHTS have a tendency to punish those who have hurt them. Rm 12: 14-21. This passage about do-ing good for the persecutor could be prayed with great profit by an EIGHT.

5. EIGHTS have as a first response to a request the answer "No." They need this "No" to get time to see what they would really like to do. Mt 21: 28-32. A call to rethink an initial response.

6. EIGHTS can make immediate and spon-taneous judgments without taking time to get the full picture. Ps 46:10. An invitation to be still and know God and hopefully in this stillness before God the person will come to see a situation in its depths and fullness.

7. EIGHTS find it difficult to really listen. Ps

32:8-9. This is God's promise to instruct the person and also the warning not to be senseless.

8. EIGHTS can be full of ideas about a project and even though they have heard advice can quickly forget it. Ac 5:27-33. Can be helpful here. Obedience to the Spirit of God is more important than following one's own projects.

9. EIGHTS can be so sensitive to injustice that they see power plays where there are none. Ps 37. Can be a reminder that the fate of the virtuous and the wicked is in God's hands and not theirs. It is a call to a more innocent approach to life and relationships.

10. EIGHTS can be punishing, debunking, and cut others down to size. 2 Tm 4:1-5. A call to unfailing patience in teaching and leading others forward.

11. EIGHTS have anger that is intense, immediate. Lk 22: 47-51. Jesus' response to such anger.

12. EIGHTS love to be involved in stimulating and even dangerous activities. Life can be boring for them if there is no stimulation. Ps 131. A call to the rest they need. The image is of a child. This childlike innocence is what they most need to cultivate.

13. EIGHTS see sin as all black. They find it well nigh impossible to experience being the loved sinner. Ep 2:1-10. A beautiful expression of the generous mercy of God.

14. EIGHTS can exhaust others with their long, hard work and the expectations that others be as they are. Lk 10: 38-42. The Martha and Mary scene that would be a good passage for these persons.

15. EIGHTS want to keep things moving and often run over others to achieve what they consider important. Mk 10: 13-16. Jesus and the children

shows the tenderness of Jesus toward the little ones, the seemingly insignificant. The desire to send them away that is expressed by the disciples occasions an important teaching for the number EIGHT.

16. EIGHTS have been called: "The sandpaper of the Enneagram." They can be abrasive and sarcastic. 2 Tm 2: 23-25. Teaches them to have nothing to do with stupid, senseless quarrels, but to correct others in a spirit of gentleness.

17. EIGHTS have for all their apparent strength, a deep-seated fear of themselves, particularly of their own anger and also a fear of death. Jn 6:25-58. Can put them in touch with God's gift of eternal life.

18. EIGHTS appear not to need others. The letter to Philemon is all about the value of laboring together for the Gospel. It shows in one forum the value of team enterprise.

19. EIGHTS are in control, even in their affective lives. Mk 10:17-22. The story of the rich young man. Jesus looked on him and loved him, but loved enough to let the young man be free to make his own choices.

20. EIGHTS find it hard to trust themselves and can be full of self-accusations. Jr 10:23-24. The prayer of Jeremiah that God would correct him, but do it gently, can be helpful.

21. EIGHTS are judgmental of others and claim their own power in the face of others' weakness. 2 Cor 5: 16-21. Teaches one not to judge by human standards, but by God's word. The call is there to become the "goodness of God."

22. EIGHTS have guilt feelings for not fighting for truth and justice. I Cor 13: 1-13. Reminds the

believer that the greatest gift is love.

23. EIGHTS have a passion for truth, love and excess. Ep 5:15-20. A call not to be thoughtless, but to recognize God's will even though it might be a wicked age in which we live.

24. EIGHTS have difficulty admitting pain, weakness and need for love. They also find it difficult to be vulnerable and to care for themselves. 2 Cor 12:7-10. A reminder of God's grace at work in their weakness. It is a beautiful statement of the acceptability of human weakness and powerlessness.

25. EIGHTS want power. Lk 22:24-27. The one who is the greatest is the one who serves.

26. EIGHTS like to win. 2 Tm 4:6-8. I have fought the good fight. Winning isn't the issue.

27. EIGHTS hate themselves for being weak or feeling discouraged. Lk 22:31-34. I have prayed for you. Let Jesus pray for you too, if you are a number EIGHT.

28. EIGHTS can capitalize on another's weakness to win. Jr 17:3-10. Trust in God not in others.

29. EIGHTS know the eye for an eye temptation. Mt 5:38-42. Speaks directly to this point.

30. EIGHTS have revenge as a temptation. They want to teach the person who has failed and let them pick up their own pieces. Jn 18: 25-27. Peter's denial might put them in touch with their own possibilities of sinning: what that feels like and what is needed in the weak moments of life.

Giftedness To Rejoice In And Strengthen In Prayer...

1. EIGHTS are at home in a difficult situation. 2 Cor 4. Eights are conscious of the treasure within and have a willingness to give themselves even in difficulty. Prayer with this passage can be very affirming of the gift of courageous generosity.

2. EIGHTS are selfless and do not think of counting the cost as they enter into a project. 2 Cor 6:3-10. Affirms this way of being. God's servants are proven by great fortitude in suffering.

3. EIGHTS have a sense of their own people and of blood kinship. Jn 10:14-16. Portrays Jesus with a kind of love that is willing to lay down his life for his loved ones.

4. EIGHTS are marked by directness and an uncomplicated approach to life. Mt 5:37. Asks all to be direct and uncomplicated. "Say yes if you mean yes and no if you mean no."

5. EIGHTS have a capacity for making others feel secure around them, and also happy. Ph 4:4-9. Speaks Paul's desires for the same gifts for his followers.

6. EIGHTS possess an ability to rally people and communicate vision. Lk 4:16-22. Shows Jesus doing just that.

7. EIGHTS are optimistic. I P 3:15. Hope is acknowledged and there is a call to be prepared to make a defense for the hope that is in us.

8. EIGHTS encourage growth and independence in others. 2 Tm 3:10-17. The description of the formation of young Timothy can have resonances for the natural desires and gifts of these persons.

9. EIGHTS set great importance in equality of persons. Ac 4:32-35. The early Christian community held all things in common. No person lacked what was necessary while another had more than enough.

10. EIGHTS have a sense of life, of hard work. They play hard. 2 Cor 11: 1-33. Praises and calls for the hard work that is natural to them.

11. EIGHTS are capable of loving deeply. Ph 1:3-5. A prayer of thanksgiving that can be offered for the persons that they feel deeply grateful for and who are loved by them.

12. EIGHTS possess a tenderness and innocence that is most often only evident in the presence of children, animals, nature or the weak. Pray with Ps 104 and the glories of creation can release this tenderness.

13. EIGHTS feel deeply the suffering of the world and the poor. Ps 34. Can put them in touch with God's justice and love. It is a call to praise these attributes in God that they so often find lacking in human relationships.

14. EIGHTS are honest. Gn 3:9. Poses a stark question: "Where are you?" It is a question the EIGHTS could use with profit before God and would help name their feelings and situate themselves honestly in prayer.

15. EIGHTS have a real desire to improve the world and not leave it broken and divided. They can relate well to the mission of the prophet in Is 61.

16. EIGHTS are strong and often give others the message: "Lean on me." Jn 21:9-19. An invitation to let another be for them also. There will be times of diminishment, like those experienced in the aging pro-

cess, that will not allow the EIGHT to give this gift. This passage will be a call to let another be the strong one for them.

17. EIGHTS are authentic nurturers. Is 55: 1-3. A description of God's nurturance of His/Her people.

18. EIGHTS are direct. They can feel very strengthened in their ability to name things by reading and praying the prophetic books of Amos and Joel.

19. EIGHTS are courageous. I P 4:12-19. A call to courage to share in Christ's suffering.

20. The EIGHTS' word is their bond. Is 6:8-9. Isaiah's word was his bond. I will go. Send me.

21. EIGHTS live in reality and the present moment. They have the capacity to say, Yes, there is a problem, and to do something about it. Jn 2:13-25. Jesus cleanses the Temple. He realized there was a problem and did something about it.

22. EIGHTS have an intensity and energy about them. Jn 9:4-5. Shows the same energy and intensity present in Jesus. As long as the day lasts, I work.

23. EIGHTS are generous. Si 29:8-17. A reflection on generosity.

24. EIGHTS love a challenge and are at home in a difficult situation. Mt 14: 22-33. The account of Jesus walking on the water.

SCRIPTURE FOR THE NUMBER NINE

Sinfulness To Pray Through . . .

1. NINES repress feelings and often appear drained of energy. Rv 3:14-16. Expresses the desire on

God's part for a full involvement of self in faith and life.

2. It can be difficult to get NINES to move. Ac 10:1-20. Expresses the commission to preach and to bear witness.

3. NINES' manner of speaking can be monotonous. They can be constant complainers. Col 3: 12-17. The call to dedicate oneself to thankfulness, to look more at the gift of life and faith.

4. NINES often attempt to get others to do their work. Lk 1:39-45. Mary's willingness to reach out to serve her cousin at a time when it would have seemed that she could have expected the service of others.

5. NINES can lose the larger picture of a situation because of their concern with details. Lk 17:11-19. The story of the cure of the ten lepers. The unexpressed gratitude that is in the scene shows what can happen when the truth of a situation is obscured.

6. NINES avoid conflict. Jn 7:1-38. Jesus enters into conflict fearlessly.

7. NINES can be over involved in trivia. Rm 11:33-36. A call to understand the depths of the mystery of God.

8. NINES can experience the outer world as not caring for them and this leads to an unwillingness to conform to social standards. Lk 2:1-7. Human uncaring caused suffering for the Holy Family.

9. NINES find it hard to say Yes or No in a given situation and to stand up against hard demands. Jn 15:18-27. Helps the NINE to know that persecution is to be expected in life and that one does not face it alone.

10. NINES know the experience of hopelessness

at times. Mt 21: 8-22. The promise of prayer being answered if there is faith.

11. NINES resign themselves to things the way they are. Mt 25:31-46. The last judgment scene. We will be judged on response to the world's needs.

12. NINES look for meaning outside themselves instead of undertaking the inner journey. Lk 17:20-21. The Kingdom of God is right here.

13. NINES know an inner paralysis that leads to indecision. Mt 25:14-30. Parable of the talents. There is in it a powerful commentary on lost opportunity.

14. NINES don't take responsibility for their lives. Jn 5:1-9. The story of the paralytic at the pool. He waited thirty-eight years for someone else to come.

15. NINES don't feel important or believe that they matter. I Cor 12: 12-30. All the members of the body are vital.

16. NINES can give even those they love the feeling that there is nothing special about them. Their emotions are suppressed. Jn 11:17-44. Puts us in touch with the strong emotional tone of Jesus' personality and his comfortability showing his emotions.

17. NINES can expect those they love strongly to give them their meaning and importance and hence become hysterical and clinging. Jn 20: 11-18. Recounts Jesus' command to Mary of Magdala that she not cling to him.

18. NINES do not handle strong feelings well. Heb 5:7-10. Recounts the variety of feelings that were part of the human journey of Jesus.

19. NINES are forgetful. Heb 6:9-12. The expression of God's remembrance of human goodness

and the call to persevere in goodness.

20. NINES can be unconcerned with things not immediately present. Heb 3:15-19. Expresses the importance of the present moment.

21. NINES can be experienced as "really on" or "really off." Jn 15:1-9. A call to consistency. Remain on the branch bearing fruit.

22. NINES are not concerned with the future. Jn 17. Jesus' concern for the future of his apostles. He prays for their needs.

23. NINES are sensual and often feel guilty about this, particularly their struggles with their lusts. Lk 7:36-50. Jesus loves and forgives the adulterous woman.

24. NINES in their effort to protect themselves from expressing strong feelings can be cold, or stiff. Lk 13:34-35. Shows Jesus lamenting openly over Jerusalem. He does not hide his strong feelings.

25. NINES are not punctual. Ps 40. A Psalm of waiting for God. The NINE can touch into their own experience of waiting and come to understand better what it means for them to keep others waiting.

26. NINES can forget detail. Mk 8: 1-10. At the multiplication of the loaves and fish there is the attention to the fragments.

27. NINES have a tendency to be lazy. Pr 6:6-11. The story of the idler and the ant!

28. NINES lack purpose. 2 Tm 1:6-14. A reminder to stir into a flame the gift of God.

29. NINES are stubborn. Ex 33:1-4. The plight of the stiffnecked Israelites.

30. NINES have a low level of awareness and become easily bored. Lk 1:46-55. Praying the

Magnificat can keep alive the awareness of God's presence and gifting.

31. NINES can be perceived as selfish and involved with only about 1% of themselves. Jn 21: 15-17. The reminder that love is proved in service of the other.

32. NINES are hoarders. Mt 6:19-21. Do not lay up treasures.

33. NINES go very much according to their likes and dislikes. Jm 2:1-4. Sets forth two standards of judgments.

34. NINES are procrastinators. Lk 14:15-24. The invited guests lose their chance to enter the Kingdom because of their willingness to make excuses.

Giftedness To Rejoice In And Strengthen In Prayer . . .

1. NINES are the peacemakers of the Enneagram. Ep 2:14-18. Christ is our peace.

2. NINES are unflappable and accepting of others. Jn 8:2-11. Recounts Jesus' unflappable and accepting attitude with the adultress.

3. NINES are non-judgmental. Rm 14:7-12. We belong to the Lord and should not pass judgment on each other.

4. NINES are fair and can usually appreciate both sides of a situation. Ps 15. Praises the person who does no wrong to the neighbor.

5. NINES are the salt of the earth type personalities and in their giftedness can be very present to the now moment. Mt 6:25-34. Trust in providence. Living in the present securely.

6. NINES possess a quality of genuine

groundedness. Col 2:6-7. Be rooted in God.

7. NINES have the gift of speaking a hard truth in a matter of fact way. 2 Cor 4:1-6. Speaks of the gift of honest, simple proclamation.

8. NINES are calm and can reassure others. Jn 2:1-12. Mary's concern and reassurance of another. She remains calm even in the face of Jesus' seeming rebuke of her request.

9. NINES have a sense of harmony or union with the world and others. Jn 17:20-26. Jesus' prayer that all may be one. It is a prayer close to the heart of a NINE.

10. NINES are undemanding and easy to be with. 1 P 2:1-3. The command not to be hard on others.

11. NINES are balanced. Ep 5:1-20. The call to keep a careful watch over one's conduct.

12. NINES are approachable. Ga 5:13-15. Place yourselves at the service of one another.

13. NINES are concerned for unity and harmony. Jm 4:1-3. An expression of great concern for unity.

14. NINES are gentle. Mt 11:28-30. Learn from me for I am gentle.

15. NINES are non-conformists with the ability to go against the stream when they need to. Mt 15:10-20. Jesus' words on what is clean and unclean, on the difference between the inside and the outside.

16. NINES are modest. Ep 4:7-16. Each of us has received God's favor in the manner God bestows it.

17. NINES are relaxed. Jn 4:5-26. The relaxation of Jesus with the woman of Samaria.

18. NINES are kindly. 2 Tm 2:22-26. Be kindly toward all.

19. NINES are unselfconscious. Lk 21: 1-4. Widow's mite. The woman's unawareness of the magnitude of her gift.

20. NINES make others feel important. Lk 19:1-10. The searching out of what is lost.

SCRIPTURE FOR THE NUMBER ONE

Sinfulness To Pray Through . . .

1. ONES are preoccupied with the imperfection around them and within themselves. Mt 13:24-30. Parable of weeds. Jesus challenges them to let weeds and wheat grow together until the harvest.

2. ONES tend to dream impossible dreams. Ph 3:6-10. Paul faces the limits of his impossible dream of perfection by his own righteousness.

3. ONES are resentful. They repress their anger. Lk 15:25-32. Parable of elder son. In anger the elder son denies ties to his brother and refuses to go into the feast.

4. ONES constantly find fault and notice what is lacking. Ga 6:1-5. Christians are to do good and bear one another's burdens.

5. ONES have a drivenness about them, a restless striving and no inner serenity. Mk 4:26-29. Parable of seed growing secretly. Relax, growth of reign of God is happening.

6. ONES can be obsessed with minutiae. Mt 23:23-24. Jesus warns scribes and pharisees who are exacting in small things, but miss the more important:

justice, mercy and good faith.

7. ONES constantly rehash and hold many post-mortems when things go wrong. Is 38:17. Cast wrongs behind your back; God forgets even sin.

8. ONES can be picky and always fighting sloppiness in all areas of life. Jn 8:1-11. Jesus looks with compassion on the woman caught in adultery and not with the glaring eyes of the righteous.

9. ONES are always qualifying their statements and lack flow and naturalness with life. Mt 25:14-30. Parable of talents. Constant measuring of self is like burying the gift.

10. ONES are judgmental, look at things in terms of good or bad, right or wrong, or are moralizing. Mt 7:1-5. On Judging. Jesus uses strong words about judging others.

11. ONES are overly analytical, often pondering the why of things. Is 55:8-9. God's thoughts and ways are mysterious and so is human life.

12. ONES are argumentative. Ga 5:19-21. Paul corrects this attitude as a work of self-indulgence.

13. ONES are harsh towards others in their criticism. Jm 2:12-13. Judgment without mercy will be offered those who show no mercy.

14. ONES have an ability to just let things be. Lk 1:26-38. Annunciation. Mary surrenders to God's plan in her life.

15. ONES are passive aggressive rather than express anger directly. Mt 5:38-42. Jesus calls them to turn the other cheek.

16. ONES say "yes" too quickly and then resent it. II Cor 9:7-8. Free giving is what counts and not simply pleasing others.

17. ONES have explosive anger. Mt 5:43-44. Jesus commands love of the enemy.

18. ONES are ruled by the expectations of others. They worry excessively. Mk 5:25-34. Cure of woman with a hemorrhage. She freely comes to touch Jesus despite social pressure.

19. ONES are constantly critical and finding fault with themselves. Lk 5:27-32. Jesus calls a tax collector and eats with sinners.

20. ONES find it hard to receive compliments as they feel that they do not deserve them. Lk 15:11-32. Prodigal son. The father does not treat the son as he deserves, but rather as a son.

21. ONES experience a great deal of disappointment. Things are not what they could be. Rm 8:31-39. God's love for them and the world is unshakable and calls for hope.

22. ONES are restless and have a desire to move on to some other place or something else. Heb 2:14-18. Jesus, the compassionate and trustworthy high priest, fully identified with humanity.

23. ONES don't like to be tied down. Heb 12:1-4. Example of Jesus whose fidelity they need to keep in sight.

24. ONES do not like being in a position with others' dependent on them. They find the parental role difficult. Ez 34:1-16. God reproves the leaders (Shepherds) for failing to be responsible, healing and nurturing.

25. ONES speak with an edge in their voice. They are at odds with reality. Jm 5:7-8. This passage calls them to be patient with reality just as the farmer waits for rain.

26. ONES can easily ridicule, for nothing is as it should be. Gn 1: 1-2, 4. God saw that creation was good.

27. ONES can feel guilty for being human. Jn 13:1-11. Jesus washes the disciples' feet. Can they let him wash their feet? Or must they clean them first?

28. ONES dread criticism. To fend it off they will criticize themselves first. I Cor 4:1-5. Paul challenges power given to others' criticism and relinquishes judgment of self, for God is judge.

29. ONES cringe when scolded. Mt 6:19-21. True Treasure. Jesus challenges them to be attached in heart to the True Treasure.

30. ONES are forever apologizing. They take great pains to make things clear even when it isn't necessary. 2 Cor 11:30-33. Paul finds boasting foolish. Be with the image of the escape of Paul: lowered in a basket from a window set in the outer wall of the town.

31. ONES find it difficult to acknowledge their gifts. I Cor 12:4-11. Paul says that gifts are from God.

32. ONES are jealous. I Cor 13:4. Love is not jealous.

33. ONES are misers with time. Mk 6:30-34. Jesus seeks solitude, but allows the need of the crowd to take his person and time.

Giftedness To Rejoice In And Strengthen In Prayer . . .

1. ONES have great idealism. They desire a world full of truth, love and justice. Mt 5:1-12. The Beatitudes.

2. ONES strive to do things well. Ph 3:7-16. Paul describes his pursuit of perfection in Christ.

3. ONES are scrupulously honest and fair. They have a keen sense of fairness and are straightforward in speech. Mk 3: 1-6. Jesus cures the man with the withered hand.

4. ONES have a capacity to inspire others. They are endowed with a divine restlessness which goads them on to do good. Ph 2:1-5. Paul urges unity in love and humility.

5. ONES are gifted with leadership qualities. Mk 10:35-45. Jesus describes leadership as service and not being in the first place.

6. ONES make good teachers. They have good insight. Jn 4: 1-42. Jesus and the Samaritan woman.

7. ONES can be critical and name what is genuinely wrong. Mk 7:1-13. Jesus critiques the traditions of the pharisees.

8. ONES can be challenging and stimulating. Mk 11: 15-19. The cleansing of the Temple.

9. ONES find serenity when they are converted. 2 Cor 12:7-10. Paul's prayer: "My grace is enough for you."

10. ONES have an ability to see others' giftedness and enable it. Mk 1: 16-20. Call of disciples.

11. ONES are blessed with high energy and great intensity. Mk 1:14-34. The first or typical day in the mission of Jesus.

12. ONES make good missionaries or preachers. I Tm 4:12-16. Paul urges Timothy (and them) to fan the spiritual gift.

13. ONES have the gift of perseverance. Mt

10:17-25. Trials of the disciples: Spirit will speak through them.

14. ONES have a sense of loyalty. Jn 10:1-18. The Good Shepherd. Jesus lays down his life for his own.

15. ONES are stable and level-headed. Lk 9: 51-56. Jesus rebukes the "sons of thunder" who would call down fire from heaven on the inhospitable Samaritan town.

16. ONES have a keen sense of justice and charity. Mi 6:8. God wants justice, tenderness and humility.

17. ONES are defenders of the downtrodden and the common cause. Lk 4:16-22. Jesus at Nazareth describes his mission as "Good News for the Poor."

18. ONES are altruistic. Lk 9:10-17. Jesus heals and feeds the crowd with bread.

19. ONES are high principled. Ga 2:11-21. Paul confronts Peter over his not eating with Gentiles and proclaims the Gospel principle of faith in Jesus.

20. ONES are sensible and have the capability of blending the real and the ideal. Mt 15:21-28. Jesus responds favorably to the Canaanite woman's plea to extend his healing power beyond Israel.

21. ONES have a sense of perspective enabling them to view a problem or a situation as a whole. I K 3: 4-9. Solomon's prayer for a discerning heart.

22. ONES are dependable. Mk 1: 40-45. Jesus wants to cure the leper and does so.

FOOTNOTES

Chapter I

1. The reader can pursue the study of the Enneagram Personality study in a basic workshop. Also a helpful tool with it is the following work: Maria Beesing, O.P., Robert J. Nogosek, C.S.C. and Patrick H. O'Leary, S.J., *The Enneagram: A Journey of Self Discovery* (Denville, NJ: Dimension Books, Inc., 1984).

2. Dag Hammarskjold, *Markings.* Trans. by Leif Sjoberg and W.H. Auden (New York: Ballantine Books, 1964), p. 48.

3. Teilhard de Chardin, S.J., *The Divine Milieu* (New York: Harper Torchbooks, 1965), pp. 76-78.

4. Claudio Naranjo and Robert E. Ornstein, *On the Psychology of Meditation* (New York: The Viking Press, 1979), pp. 170ff.

5. Robert N. Bellah, Richard Madsen, William M. Sullivan, Ann Swidler, and Steven M. Tipton, *Habits of the Heart* (New York: Harper and Row, Pub., 1985).

6. For further reflections on this, see William Johnston, *Silent Music* (San Francisco: Harper and Row, Pub., 1976), pp. 134-138.

Chapter III

1. Paul V. Robb, S.J., "Conversion as a Human Experience," *Studies in the Spirituality of the Jesuits.* Vol. XIV. May, 1986. No. 3. p. 25.

2. Ibid. p. 7.

Chapter IV

1. Our own reflection has been aided by the work of Naranjo and Ornstein, *On the Psychology of Meditation.* They studied Eastern forms of prayer and described three different paths of centering. We have made application of this to Christian Spirituality and the Enneagram Personality Study.

2. Ibid. c. 2. See also William Johnston, *Christian Mysticism Today* (San Francisco: Harper and Row, Pub., 1984), pp. 105-115 for a discussion on Eucharistic symbolism.

Chapter V

1. Evelyn Eaton Whitehead and James D. Whitehead, *Seasons of Strength* (Garden City: Image Books, A Division of Doubleday and Company, Inc., 1986), p. 101.

2. Brother David Steindl-Rast, *Gratefulness, the Heart of Prayer* (New York: Paulist Press, 1986), p. 181.

3. Naranjo, *On the Psychology of Meditation,* p. 115.

4. Ibid. p. 117.

5. Ibid. p. 129.

6. Ibid. p. 129.

7. Louis M. Savary, Patricia H. Berne and Strephon Kaplan Williams, *Dreams and Spiritual Growth: A Christian Approach to Dreamwork* (New York: Paulist Press, pp. 22-24.

8. John A. Sanford, *Dreams and Healing* (New York: Paulist Press, 1978).

Chapter VI

1. St. Teresa of Avila, *The Way of Perfection* in *The Collected Works of St. Teresa of Avila,* Vol. II, trans. by Kieran Kavanaugh, O.C.D. and Otilio Rodriguez, O.C.D. (Washington, D.C.:ICS Publications, 1980), c. 26, nos. 1-3, pp. 133-134.

2. *The Cloud of Unknowing and The Book of Privy Counseling,* ed. by William Johnston (New York: Image Books, Doubleday and Co. Inc., 1973(c. 3 p. 48.

3. Ibid. c. 4, p. 52.

4. Ibid. c. 7, p. 56.

5. Anthony de Mello, S.J., *Sadhana: A Way to God* (St. Louis: The Institute of Jesuit Sources, 1978), p. 27.

6. Quoted in Naranjo, *On the Psychology of Meditation,* p. 80.

7. Antoine De Saint-Exupery, *The Little Prince,* trans. by Katherine Woods (New York: Reynal and Hitchcok, 1943), p. 65.

8. Ibid. p. 66.

9. Ibid. p. 67

10. Ibid. pp. 67-68.

11. Ibid. p. 72.

Appendix I

1. C.G. Jung, *Two Essays on Analytical Psychology,* in *Collected Works,* Vol. 7, 2d. ed. (Princeton, NJ: Princeton University Press, 1966).

2. Ira Progoff, *At a Journal Workshop* (New York: Dialogue House Library, 1975), pp. 158ff.

3. Ibid. pp. 77ff.

Appendix II

1. Rollo May, *Man's Search for Himself* (New York: Signet Books pub. by The New American Library, Inc., 1967), pp. 30-40.

Appendix III

1. Louis M. Savary and Patricia H. Berne, *Prayerways* (San Francisco: Harper and Row, Pub., 1980), pp. 147-155.

2. See Appendix I for the naming of the Idealizations and Appendix V for the listing of the gifts of the personality types. For the theory, consult Beesing, Nogosek and O'Leary, *The Enneagram: A Journey of Self Discovery,* pp. 156-171.